Action-Packed Classrooms
Movement Strategies
to Invigorate
K–5 Learners

Acknowledgements

Thank You, God, for allowing me to be Your vehicle through *Action-Packed Classrooms*. I am truly blessed.

Action-Packed Classrooms is written in the forever loving spirit of my Dad, who taught me to never settle for less than my best. And for you, Mom, I love you.

Action-Packed Classrooms is written in honor of and as a tribute to all teachers who are out in the trenches making a difference in the lives of kids. There is no other profession that has such a lasting impact on children.

Action-Packed Classrooms is dedicated to Harry V. Redinger, for without your expertise, guidance, and support this project could not have conveyed the message of movement and learning so effectively. You are such a gift and I am forever grateful you have entered and are completing my Action-Packed Life.

Action-Packed Classrooms
Movement Strategies
to Invigorate
K–5 Learners

Cathie Summerford

THE BRAIN STORE
Resources for Growing Minds ®

San Diego, CA USA

For information:
The Brain Store, Inc.
4202 Sorrento Valley Blvd., Ste. B
San Diego, California 92121
E-mail: info@thebrainstore.com

Printed in the United States of America

Library of Congress Cataloging-in-Publication Data

Summerford, Cathie, 1957—
Action-packed classrooms : movement strategies to invigorate the learning process/ by Cathie Summerford.

   p.   cm.

Includes bibliographical references.
ISBN 1-890460-45-1 (pbk. : alk. paper)

1. Movement education. 2. Learning--Physiological aspects. 3. Cognition in children. I. Title.

GV452.S76 2005
372.86'8--dc22

2005014046

This book is printed on acid-free paper.

3 5 7 9 10 8 6 4 2

Editorial Director: Deborah Ness Edwards
Editor: Karen Miller
Cover Design: Sarah Hedricks
Interior Design: Cheryl Ann Harrison
Production Artist: Rusty von Dyl
Proofreader: Katie Franco

Table of Contents

Foreword

Recent research into how the human brain operates clearly indicates that students must be fully engaged in the learning process—physically, emotionally, and intellectually—for maximum results. Yet this idea should come as little or no surprise to anyone with significant experience in education. Involve them and they will understand information better and remember it longer. The critical difference is that we now have scientific proof that the best learning occurs when students are actively engaged with the material. This growing body of evidence dramatically increases the urgency of the present situation and tells us that educators must immediately begin developing instructional techniques that will more effectively address this critical aspect of learning.

However, it is one thing to understand the importance of this issue theoretically and a completely different one to decipher how to put this into practice. What we need so desperately is to find the "translators"—individuals with a thorough knowledge of the academic issues involved, yet who are also steeped in practical classroom experience. It is these people who will ultimately be able to best synthesize these well-researched ideas into specific techniques educators can put to use in their classrooms tomorrow. The importance of this step to turning research into practice cannot be overstated. It lies at the heart of increasing the effectiveness of every classroom, improving our school systems, and ultimately maintaining the strength of our nation.

We are therefore extremely fortunate to have a few excellent educators dedicating their lives to the advancement of this important cause, offering us their insights regarding how they have been able to bring these theoretical concepts into everyday practice. Cathie Summerford is one of these rare individuals, and *Action-Packed Classrooms* is essentially a gift she is offering us. Based on her lifetime of study regarding how students learn best and a strong desire to make classrooms more dynamic and effective, she has developed a remarkable text. The ideas presented here provide concise guidance to teachers wishing to incorporate increased levels of physical activity into their own classrooms, and the background information she offers is clearly presented and easy to understand. Consequently the argument she makes is impossible to ignore—we must add more physical activity to almost every aspect of learning.

It is my sincere hope that, as educators use this book as a guide to enhancing their own lessons, they will also begin to think differently about how they approach all aspects of the learning process. The ideas should provoke profound consideration on how we are currently conducting our classrooms and how we might be able to improve them in the future. It is exactly that kind of book—a fundamental breakthrough in how to approach effective classroom instruction—that should expand the boundaries of our present thinking about how all classroom lessons are designed and conducted.

—Dr. Rich Allen, author of
*Impact Teaching: Ideas and Strategies for Teachers
to Maximize Student Learning*

Author's Welcome

You are about to embark on a journey that will undoubtedly have a positive impact on your teaching and your students' learning. There is no honor greater than to touch the direction and potential of another's life. This is especially true in education at a time when children are the most impressionable. Engaging their bodies and minds is more productive than delivering a non-interactive lecture to them; bringing movement into the classroom works!

Action and movement stimulate the body, which in turn stimulates the brain and a person's ability to learn and retain information. The strategies and techniques presented in *Action-Packed Classrooms* are founded on scientific research about the link between movement and cognition. If you bring energy into your classroom, your students will be motivated and able to retain more information. Using physical movement for optimal learning in your classroom and at your school is a no-brainer (if you'll pardon the pun) and should be a standard requirement for educators of every level.

It really is easy to add action-packed lessons to your classroom routine. But if you are unsure about your ability to implement motion and excitement on a regular basis, team up with a colleague (or your entire faculty) for support. You can help each other master the skills that will optimize learning for your students. Embracing these ideas and using these strategies will also energize you. Rediscover the joy of teaching!

Good luck and have fun,

Cathie Summerford

Introduction

Evidence is mounting that each person's capacity to master new and remember old information is improved by biological changes in the brain brought on by physical activity.
  —Dr. John Ratey, *A User's Guide to the Brain*

The state of public education has been the subject of consternation for many decades. The current standards and assessment movement is only the most recent of many attempts by public officials to effect change in a distressed system. The question that needs answering, however, is not how to motivate teachers to teach properly, but how they should teach differently in order for children to learn. How do children learn and therefore, by making use of the diverse resources at our disposal, how should we teach? In an effort to utilize cutting-edge educational information, this book will apply brain-based research in order to show the effectiveness of creating an action-packed classroom for the success of all learners.

Why Read *Action-Packed Classrooms?*

1. To understand the research behind movement and learning
2. To learn strategies to anchor learning in any classroom
3. To gain knowledge of movement-based activities for intrinsic learning
4. To create an action plan for immediately implementing these techniques in your classroom

Brain-based research has been the subject of scientific study since the mid-1800s, when Hitzig and Fritsch first discovered that the areas of the brain responsible for movement could be located in the cerebral cortex. Still, the results of this fascinating field of research, which have such diverse applications in the field of education, have not yet found their way into general practice. Despite the fact that numerous studies have consistently proven that programs focusing on movement, creativity, and physical education classes focusing on healthy skills for life are more effective than discipline or standards in effecting achievement, special subjects continue to be dropped from curriculums in favor of extra practice in basic skills (Kearney, 1996). The current educational system is neither making effective use of the resources available nor putting into practice the volumes of relevant research that could make a difference in what our children learn.

This country has developed a very rich, visual, mobile, multicultural society with readily available access to cutting-edge research in scientific fields. Brain research demonstrates that our bodies and brains are inherently connected and that no single organ has one unilateral purpose, but schools are still failing to make full use of moving mediums in instructional practice.

Most recently, studies of brain-based learning have shown that exercise can increase cognitive ability in children. This has specific applications for the field of education and draws into discussion such questions as how an increasingly sedentary lifestyle in this country is affecting its youth. It also brings into question current methodology for dealing with attention deficit disorder and whether or not these interventions are on par with what we know about the brain (Hannaford, 1995).

Despite the extraordinary quantity and quality of brain-based research that calls for motion activities to be utilized in the instructional setting, these types of activities are not being consistently implemented in classroom practice. The purpose of *Action-Packed Classrooms* is to show that research supports merging movement with academics in the classroom. The lessons, strategies, ideas, and games presented in this book are easy to implement and will help ensure that research finally finds a consistent place in education.

© Jean-Michel Cornet

Using Movement in the Classroom

Mrs. Wilson

Mrs. Wilson, a fourth grade teacher in Fontana, California, prepares for yet another lesson at Coleman Elementary School. Her day never has any dull moments because she teaches math, language arts, science, social studies, and P. E. (as well as covering recess duty). All of this stuff to do and no time to fit it all in! Anyway, who really has time to teach P. E. with all the emphasis on standardized testing? "When every minute counts, there just isn't any time for frill," she says to herself as she frantically prepares materials for the day's lesson. "How can I possibly get to all of the standards that need to be taught—not just covered—for the state of California? And if it's not on the test, why address it?"

On top of that, her twenty-eight students are very diverse and come from many cultures and backgrounds. Two new students to her class don't speak any English at all. Also, several of the children are classified as ADD/ADHD and need constant attention to stay on task.

Mrs. Wilson has come to the conclusion that if she can just keep them in their seats, focused on their work, and quiet, her mission will be accomplished! The thought of them getting up, moving around, and physically interacting only presents a vision of chaos. Mrs. Wilson does not want to lose control of what she is used to doing so she only teaches inside her comfort zone. It's been working for twenty years, after all.

Take a moment to reflect on Mrs. Wilson's situation. What she should honestly ask herself is if her approach provides effective strategies for learning. Are her students engaged in the learning process? Are there more successful and fun approaches to teaching and learning with them? Now reflect on the teachers at your school: Are you a Mrs. Wilson?

Movement facilitates cognition by
✔ anchoring learning through the body
✔ energizing and integrating the body and brain for optimal learning
✔ making learning fun

Movement in the academic classroom is essential to keeping kids focused, excited, enthusiastic, and ready to learn—all without losing control of your class. Our brains and bodies are not designed to sit down, shut up, and stay focused for hours on end. Choosing to include more action in your curriculum will be a delightful addition to your academic learning environment.

Why Use Movement?

Depending on your objective, movement can be used for a variety of purposes: calming the environment, creating an adrenaline rush, or simply transitioning students from one lesson or activity to another. Movement can be expressed and described as being less active or very active, depending on the purpose and the intensity of the activity and the objective of the lesson. This chapter will clarify the confusion that is often associated with movement in the academic classroom and address why it is so essential in education. We will examine the differences between movement, physical activity, and exercise and explore what effects each type of movement has on the brain and academic performance.

Before you begin the process of planning movement activities, you need a thorough understanding of the purpose of movement in the academic classroom. When do you use movement? Why? What are the different levels of movement? What is "bodybrain activation"? And why is aerobic activity even mentioned in this book? Classroom teachers are not P. E. teachers! As you learn the answers to these questions, you will discover just how important it is to prime student brains for learning and how aerobic exercise is a necessary component of teaching.

Movement Anchors Learning through the Body

Imagine learning multiplication facts or practicing verbs with your body. Doesn't that sound more fun than memorizing them? We learn by doing because of procedural memory. How does this work? Without getting too technical, throughout the body are chemicals and cells that have a "memory" of their own and that become engaged by movement. Once your body knows a concept, you don't forget it! Kinesthetic learners especially appreciate and benefit from this method of learning.

Movement Energizes and Integrates the Body and Brain for Optimal Learning

As an artist needs to prepare a canvas before painting it, teachers need to prepare their children in their classrooms for optimal learning. Children are like seeds that not only need to be planted, but also nourished and tended before they can blossom. The best way for teachers to do this is to engage the energy of the whole child.

Energizers, attention-getters, and cooperative games are all effective strategies for preparing students for what comes next. Not only do they focus the mind and trigger curiosity, they can include core academic concepts as previews for what the class is about to learn. They also keep boredom at bay.

Movement Makes Learning Fun

What kid could possibly be bored when learning is fun? Think back when you were a kid: What did you have the most fun doing at school? What usually comes to mind is any event that incorporated action and movement (sadly, this was mostly recess). Why? Because people need to move!

Building on the idea that movement facilitates cognition, Carla Hannaford terms every movement a "sensory-motor event" (1995). Sensory-motor events enlist the help of our core senses (touch, sight, sound, smell, taste) in order to understand the physical world and process outside stimuli. Hannaford, along with other notable researchers such as Gardner and Sperry, challenges the assumption that experiences and actions can be categorized as either entirely physical or mental, or that one should be intrinsically valued over the other.

Know When and Why to Include Movement

There are many reasons to include movement in your classroom and many situations that would benefit with its inclusion. At times, it is advantageous to arouse learners with a heady dose of sizzling tunes and vigorous moves; at other times, students benefit from a moment to relax and focus.

1. Get Attention

Have you ever had students in your class who were there physically but maybe not mentally? Movement can be used to get their attention and focus it on the classroom activity. You can have students change seats, turn to point at an interesting or new object in the room, or even roll their pencils across a desk to swap with another person.

2. Energize and Engage

Energize and engage the learners to involve them in the learning process. Creating enthusiasm, motivation, and a sense of responsibility for their own learning is absolutely essential. If students are not interested or do not take ownership in their education, they shut down and turn off the lesson. A brisk walk around the building clears their head and invigorates their body; a discussion of an immediate benefit of the knowledge they are about to gain underscores its importance.

3. Relax and Focus

There are occasions when it is beneficial to calm students down and relax them before progressing to the next lesson. Gentle movement can accomplish this goal. Holding cross-lateral positions (the right elbow touching the left knee, for example) while listening to soothing music is just one example of a quiet posture.

4. Transition between Activities

Another important use of movement is to transition students from one lesson to another. When done effectively, opportunities for movement seamlessly flow into the breaks of a traditional classroom (i.e., sedentary) environment. For example, the following scenario uses movement to collect papers from students at the end of a test: "In ten seconds, when I say 'go,' grab your test and stand up. Go!" Play music. Pause. "Next, when I say 'go', take ten giant steps in any direction and give your test paper to the closest person. Go!" Play music. Pause. "Next, when I say 'go,' carry the test paper you are holding to a desk in the corner of the room. Leave the paper on the desk and return to your seat by walking backwards. Go!" Play music until you have collected the tests from the corners of the room.

An activity like this not only stretches out kinks in the bodies of students who have sat very still for an extended period, it adds fun and relieves the tension that lingers after a test. Students will be in a happier state of mind for the next lesson.

The quantity of movement you employ depends both on what outcome you seek and the age of your students. For example, youngsters are very active in general and need frequent, rapid opportunities to move while older students may enjoy longer durations of exercise less frequently. Each group of learners and situations are different. Assess your students and adjust your movement usage accordingly.

Not All Movement Is the Same

Classroom teachers need to understand the different kinds of movement and how they apply to academic situations. Each distinct component of movement plays a huge role in the educational process. However simple they may be, these basic definitions of movement will help you understand the research on applying it to academic learning and in the classroom.

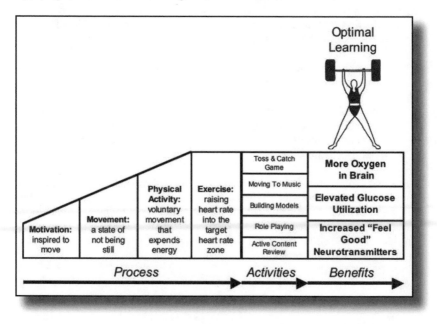

Movement

Not being stationary. For example, just the act of standing up out of a chair raises the heart rate, which changes the state of the learner. Moving the body (transitioning) from one place to another is another example of movement.

Physical Activity

Voluntary movement that is more intense or complex than basic movement. When we are physically active in a classroom, we have the opportunity to anchor learning in the body.

Exercise

Raising the heart-rate into the target heart rate zone for a minimum of twenty minutes, ideally three times per week if not more. Neuroscience is exploding with research about the benefits of exercise to cognition and general health.

Instructional methods should alternate between repetitive sedentary activities and pleasurable, movement-oriented activities because the brain's attentional system prefers high contrast, originality, and excitement. Instead of force-feeding dull and ineffective content to students, take a cue from research discoveries and include more stimulating, interactive material.

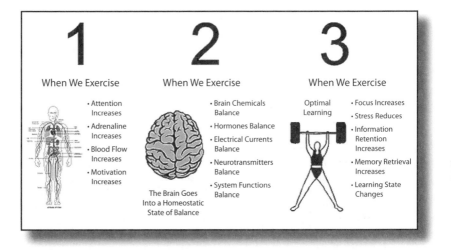

Why Is Exercise and Aerobic Activity Important to a Classroom Teacher?

Neuroscience reveals that aerobic exercise is absolutely necessary for our brains to function at top condition. With study after study in various laboratories all over the world, scientists are demonstrating that at the neuronal and cellular levels, our brains need aerobic, voluntary exercising for optimal function. In light of the increasing emphasis on standardized testing, doesn't it make sense to get the brains in top condition? Academic classroom teachers should take this "exercise thing" seriously. Physical fitness translates into cognitive fitness.

When we exercise, the body goes into high gear. Attention, adrenaline, blood flow, and motivation are elevated. Because of the increase of brain chemicals, hormones, electricity, and neurotransmitters, the entire neural system functions more efficiently. This creates a balanced, or homeostatic, state in the learner. The benefits of a homeostatic brain include better retention, stress reduction, increased memory retrieval, learning state change, and a more focused student. Aerobic recess activities and quality physical education programs provide the exercise students need.

No matter how hard they wish for it, teachers will never have the power to open up a student's head and pour information into it! Nor will they ever be in a situation when just their students' heads come to school and leave those pesky bodies at home. It seems sometimes that bodies only get in the way of learning as students become distracted and hyper and wiggle and shuffle around. And why doesn't the information teachers do manage to put inside students' heads stay there? Where does it go? It's amazing how fast students—the same little darlings who attended class every day—can forget the material.

People spend most of their time in a state in which mental and physical functioning are entwined. Whether teachers want to or not, they must include the body for true learning to occur. The following graphic demonstrates the importance of the integral entanglement and connection of the mind, body, and spirit. One does not operate or function without the others.

Working in unison and hopefully for one common goal in the educational arena, the mind, body, and spirit far exceed the capabilities of the most advanced computer programs. When functioning in full capacity, lofty goals can be reached even for learners who are traditionally hard to reach. The human brain is capable of the most amazing challenges when the whole is tapped into because the whole is greater than the sum of its parts.

Mind

The mind, or brain, is located inside the head. Instructors strive to maximize its content and efficiency.

Body

The body is everything else. Teachers frequently discount its needs and desires as less important to school and the classroom, and as one of the prime distractions to students.

Spirit

The spirit is the internal driving force that makes each one of us who we are from the core of our being. It operates within our mind and bodies.

Interestingly, some researchers theorize that an inadequate amount of movement (hypokinesis) is a possible cause or aggravating factor of ADD/ADHD. According to this theory, hyperactivity becomes a coping strategy, whereby children try to increase their focus by moving. Hyperactive children who run before class have improved their behavior so significantly that doctors were able to decrease stimulant doses in children who ran every day (Putnam, 2003). Other data support the fact that learning and mentally disabled children also display a significant positive relationship between physical activity and cognition (Sibley & Etnier, 2003). Incorporating movement into classroom instruction is considered an appropriate antidote and remedy to attention problems. Given the increasing numbers of ADHD and learning disabled children in the classroom, a group that is often highly medicated for movement issues, it is irresponsible to ignore data that many children who have been identified with attention problems have hypokinesis. Learning programs for children with ADHD or learning and mental disabilities should incorporate movement into classroom instruction.

To Summarize

Movement has significant impact on thinking and learning because it anchors an individual's thoughts and provides a framework for developmental processes. Body-centered learning should be routinely included in instruction—especially academic instruction! Integrating subject learning with active learning should be an ongoing strategy that teachers use to maximize opportunities for students to learn information.

Students who are taught that learning truly can be fun will be eager and ready for the next learning lesson. When kids have fully engaged the entire mind/body/spirit in the academic classroom, they will be ready and willing to tackle any new challenge. Furthermore, not only will the kids be enjoying their education more, their teacher will be having more fun, too!

© Jean-Michel Cornet

About the Brain and Brain Research

Principal Wallace & Mr. Sorenson

No matter how many jokes she makes about the stress that standardized testing brings to the teachers at her middle school, Principal Wallace understands that her school has to make the grade each year. Because the stakes are so high, she tries anything that seems morally, ethically, and educationally sound in order to prepare students and raise scores.

One of her most ambitious teachers, Mr. Sorenson, has lately been sharing with the rest of the staff some incredible discoveries that have been made in the field of neuroscience and how these discoveries affect our understanding of how learning takes place. Mr. Sorenson has been pushing hard for a staff development program to educate teachers about how to use this information, but Mrs. Wallace is skeptical. In the past two decades, she's seen a lot of teaching fads come and go and she isn't sure what to believe.

After a conversation about it, the two colleagues agree to investigate why another middle school performed so successfully in the last assessment. To Principal Wallace's amazement, teachers there incorporate the same research into their practice that Mr. Sorenson has been espousing. Armed with information about brain-based learning, teachers and students are energetic, enthusiastic, and eager during each school day. Mr. Sorenson's proposed staff development day becomes a "no-brainer"—Principal Wallace makes educating her staff on the practical applications of brain research a top priority. (And the rest is brain-based history.)

Making Research Work

For teachers, thriving in education means not only meeting all of the demands of the job description but also staying on top of the emerging science of how people learn. For the first time, neuroscience finally intersects with theories of learning and the evidence is clear: What happens in the brain is important to what happens in the classroom. What is thinking? What is learning? When does learning occur? How does the mind retain material? The answers to these questions relate in part to the concept of the "bodybrain."

Bodybrain—The Ultimate Multi-Tasker

What is the bodybrain? If the brain is what is inside our head and the body is all the other stuff, then the bodybrain is the combination and cooperation of both. Emerging research really relates to the interaction of both. When you think about engaging the learning experience, realize that the entire bodybrain is involved. The brain and the body influence each other.

Without a shadow of a doubt, the brain is the most complex, multi-tasking organ of the body. This single organ controls all body activities, ranging from heart rate and digestive function to emotion, learning, and memory. The brain is even thought to influence the response to disease of the immune system and to determine, in part, how well people respond to medical treatments. Ultimately, it shapes our thoughts, hopes, dreams, and imagination. In short, the brain is what makes us human.

A Short Primer on the Brain

In this chapter we will take a look at the past thirty years of evidence of the link between cognition and active engagement of the learner. The brain is a complex organ. Although all its parts and structures interact, there is a tremendous amount of specialization among its lobes and systems. The following is a short list of some of the items and terms you will encounter in the research timeline, with explanations or definitions.

Human Brain

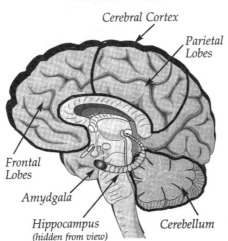

Cerebral Cortex

Parietal Lobes

Frontal Lobes

Amydgala

Hippocampus
(hidden from view)

Cerebellum

Anterior Cingulate   Located in the frontal cortex. It detects errors or unexpected results in the flow of information being processed by the rest of the brain.

Basal Ganglia   A collection of structures inside the cerebral cortex that is important to voluntary movement.

Cerebellum   Associated with movement and particularly linked to balance, posture, and gross motor skills. Located at the back and base of the brain, the cerebellum looks a little like a piece of cauliflower.

Cerebral Cortex   The wrinkled outer layer of the brain and the site of higher-level thinking and awareness. It enables people to solve problems, think critically, and make decisions.

Hippocampus   A U-shaped structure inside the brain heavily involved with the facts and details of rote and short-term memory.

Neocortex   Another term for cerebral cortex.

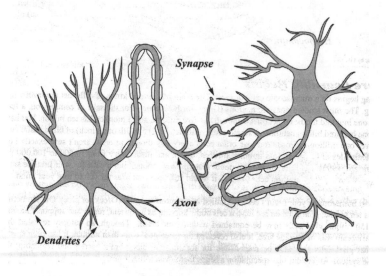

Neurogenesis   The growth of new neurons.

Neuron   A brain cell associated with learning. It has a single axon but many dendrites; neurons communicate with each other across a synapse, the space between an axon and a dendrite.

Plasticity   The ability of the brain to adapt and change throughout a person's life.

A Timeline of Research

Brain research suggests that what makes us move is also what makes us think. Current breakthroughs reveal a fundamental feature of our brains: Intelligence and learning are not processes of the brain alone, but of the entire body. We cannot separate mind and body in regard to learning.

How Movement Affects Learning:

✔ Balance improves reading capacity

✔ Exercise reduces stress

✔ Physical activity improves behavior

✔ Movement reinforces academic skills

✔ Cross-lateral movements organize brain functions

✔ Peptides aid procedural memory

✔ Eye-tracking skills and peripheral vision aid reading

Repeated research conclusively demonstrates that which should be obvious, but which is oftentimes given little consideration in education: If the body is not optimally functioning, it's hard for the brain to function, and vice-versa. Understanding how the body works and providing the resources that are necessary to maintain optimal brain functioning are essential prerequisites to learning. Developing and implementing teaching methods that employ action-packed instructional methods from numerous documented research studies have proven most effective in promoting student learning.

The field of studying the conjunction of the mind and body is not new:

1870
Eduard Hitzig & Gustav Fritsch
Discovered in experiments with dogs that areas of the brain responsible for movement could be located in the cerebral cortex.

1870
John Hughlings Jackson
Suggested the existence of a motor cortex within the cerebral hemispheres (Jankovic et al., 1997).

But just look at what scientists have learned in the past thirty years:

1972
A. Jean Ayres
Discovered a link between touch-sensitivity (inability to tolerate touch) and learning disorders in children. Her highly successful program for learning disorders deals with waking up the sensory system by appropriately activating all the touch receptors.

1973
Evelyn Lee Teng & Roger Sperry
Suggested that the brain was a means of refining motor behavior to promote survival instead of motor behaviors existing to support the activity of the brain.

1977
John Streff
Conducted a double-blind study of 538 sixth graders and determined that thirty minutes a day of motor-sensory development lowered text anxiety and incidences of myopia and raised academic success.

1977
James Prescott
Noted that the anterior cingulate is particularly active when novel movements or movement combinations are initiated. Also noted that movement impairments negatively affect the cerebellum and its connections to other parts of the brain. Experiments with rats explored the role of early motor development in the developing learner.

1977
A. G. Gilbert
Found that third graders studying language arts concepts through dance increased standardized reading scores by 13 percent in six months.

1980
David Clarke
Confirmed that physical spinning activities led to alertness, attention, and relaxation in the classroom.

1980
Lyelle Palmer
Found that hand-eye coordination tasks, spinning, tumbling, rocking, pointing, counting, jumping, and ball toss activities stimulated early neural growth patterning and showed positive effects on students through the Metropolitan Readiness Test, Test of Visual Perception, and the Otis Group Intelligence Test.

1982
Fred Martens
Revealed, in a study of more than 500 Canadian children, that students who spent an extra hour in gym class performed notably better on exams than did less active students.

1986
Judith Hooper & Dick Teresi
Found a direct link from the cerebellum to the pleasure centers in the emotional system; sensory-motor experiences (like playing during recess) feed directly into the brain's pleasure centers.

1986
Dee Coulter
Suggested that long periods of reading without relaxing the focus of the eye by gazing into the distance possibly cause inflammation and the enlargement of the eyeball, leading to myopia or near-sightedness.

1989
Richard Dienstbier
Suggested that physical exercise alone seems "to train a quick adrenaline-noradrenaline response and rapid recovery." In other words, working out with your body trains your brain to respond to challenges quickly.

1990
Black, Isaacs, Anderson, Alcantara & Greenbough

Found that rats that became proficient at the precise, coordinated movements needed to nimbly run across ropes and thin metal bridges had a greater number of connections among the neurons in their brains than did rats that were sedentary or rats that merely ran on automated wheels. Rats in the first group also had more capillaries around the brain's neurons than the sedentary rats. In the same way that exercise shapes up the muscles, heart, lungs and bones, it strengthens the basal ganglia, cerebellum, and corpus callosum, all key areas of the brain.

1991
R. E. Dustman

Found that among three test groups, study participants who partook of vigorous aerobic exercise improved short-term memory, reaction time, and creativity.

1993
Stephen Silverman

Reviewed many studies suggesting that students will boost academic learning from games and so-called "play" activities.

1994
Peter Strick & Frank Middleton

Showed that two areas of the brain that were associated solely with control of muscle movement, the basal ganglia and the cerebellum, are also important in coordinating thought. These areas are also connected to the frontal lobe area where planning the order and timing of future behaviors occurs.

1995
Susan Brink

Reported that there is tremendous value in novel motor stimulation throughout secondary school and the rest of our lives. Aerobic conditioning has also been known to assist in memory and reduce stress. Chronic stress releases the chemicals that kill neurons in the critical area of the brain for long-term memory formation, the hippocampus.

1995
Carla Hannaford

Wrote that the interaction between the brain's attentional system and incoming sensory data helps us keep our balance, turn thinking into actions, and coordinate moves. Playground games that stimulate inner ear motion like swinging, rolling and jumping have cognitive value.

1996
William Calvin

Stated that our brain creates movements by sending a deluge of nerve impulses to either the muscles or the larynx. Novel movements shift focus in the brain and engage the prefrontal cortex and the rear two-thirds of the frontal lobes—the area of the brain often used for solving problems, planning, and sequencing new things to learn and do.

1997
Ronald Kotulak

Wrote that infants deprived of stimulation from touch and physical activities may not develop the movement-pleasure link in the brain. Fewer connections are made between the cerebellum and the brain's pleasure centers. Such a child may grow up unable to experience pleasure through usual channels of pleasurable activity. As a result, the need for intense states, one of which is violence, may develop.

1997
H. Kinoshita

Wrote that exercise triggers the release of BDNF—brain-derived neurotrophic factor. This natural substance enhances cognition by boosting the ability of neurons to communicate with each other.

1997
Henning, Jacques, Kissel, Sullivan & Alteras-Webb

Found, in a study of computer operators with musculoskeletal pain, eye strain, negative mood and low productivity problems, that having workers perform body stretching every hour as part of a three-minute break dramatically improves mood and productivity, and lessens eye, leg, and foot discomfort.

1997
McKenzie, Sallis, Kolody & Faucette
Found that the use of a two-year health-related physical education program precipitated notable positive effects on academic achievement.

1997
Henrietta Leiner & Alan Leiner
Focused their research on the cerebellum, a subsection of the brain that has a significant role in posture, coordination, balance, and movement.

1998
Kesslak, So, Choi, Cotman & Gomez-Pinilla
Suggested that physical activity aids the sedentary body and learning brain by producing increased levels of brain-derived neurotrophic factor (BDNF), which promotes neuron survival and growth and protects neurons against deterioration. BDNF is also thought to play an important role in the hippocampus, the brain structure associated with spatial memory.

1998
Jacob Raber
Pointed out the detrimental effects of chronic overproduction of stress hormones, from obesity to memory deficits from Alzheimer's disease, AIDS, dementia, and depression.

1998
Kilander, Nyman, Boberg, Hansson & Lithell
Conducted a twenty-year study of 999 men linked high blood pressure and the later development of dementia. Data from a general population of healthy elderly men indicate that hypertension and associated metabolic disturbances might be susceptibility factors for cognitive disorders. The findings add support to possibilities of intervention, such as exercise, in early stages in cognitive decline.

1999
Van Praag, Christie, Sejnowski & Gage
Discovered that animals that get regular voluntary exercise on running wheels grow more new brain cells than sedentary counterparts.

2000
Anderson, Rapp, Baek, McCloskey, Coburn-Litvak & Robinson
Voluntarily exercising rats ran in running wheels attached to their cage for seven weeks and took 30 percent fewer trials to acquire criterion performance in a maze than sedentary controls.

2002
California Department of Education (CDE)
A study matched scores from 954,000 students on the Spring 2001 administration of Stanford 9 Test (SAT-9) with results of the same students' performance on the state-mandated 2001 physical fitness test and found that academic achievement is related to their levels physical fitness (Winger & Thomas, 2002).

2002
Van Praag, Schinder, Christie, Toni, Palmer & Gage
Demonstrated that newly generated cells mature into functional neurons in the adult mammalian brain.

2002
Kempermann, Gast & Gage
Found that short-term exposure of mice to an enriched environment leads to a striking increase in new neurons, along with a substantial improvement in behavioral performance. This cellular plasticity occurred in the context of significant improvements of learning parameters, exploratory behavior, and locomotor activity.

2003
Dan Ehninger & Gerd Kempermann
Reported on animal studies of the regional effects of wheel running and the effects of environmental enrichment on cell genesis in the adult neocortex. Voluntary wheel running led to a regional increase in the number of newly generated cortical cell growth.

2003
Ryan Rhodes & Kerry Courneya
Found that exercise increases the growth of new cells in the mammalian hippocampus, an important brain structure for the acquisition of new memories.

2003
Fabel, Fabel, Tam, Kaufer, Baiker, Simmons, Kuo & Palmer
Found that voluntary physical exercise stimulates neurogenesis in the adult hippocampus.

2003
Cho, Hwang, Kang, Shin, Hwang, Lim, Lee, et al.
Researched the protective effect of exercise on Alzheimer's disease in mice. Three months of treadmill exercise improved behavioral function and restored normal concentrations of cholesterol and triglycerides.

2003
Vaynman, Ying & Gomez-Pinilla
Found a basic mechanism through which exercise may promote brain plasticity in adults.

2003
Kleim, Jones & Schallert
Found that a voluntary exercise regimen may have beneficial effects to the recovery from a brain injury.

2003
Parnpiansil, Jutapakdeegul, Chentanez, & Kotchabhakdi
Found that, in rats, exercise during pregnancy may improve spatial learning in the newborn pups.

2003
Rhodes, Van Praag, Jeffrey, Girard, Mitchell, Garland & Gage
Found that exercise increases neurogenesis in the hippocampus in mice.

2003
Lu, Bao, Chen, Xia, Fan, Zhang, Pei & Ma
Demonstrated that, for rats, social environments and play can reverse the negative cognitive effects of isolation. (Isolation affects neurogenesis, spatial learning, and memory.)

2003
Brown, Cooper-Kuhn, Kempermann, Van Praag, Winkler, Gage & Kuhn
Discovered that an enriched environment and physical activity stimulate cell growth in the hippocampus.

2004
Adlard, Perreau, Engesser-Cesar & Cotman
Found that, in rats, the cognitive benefits of exercise significantly increase over time.

2004
Griesbach, Hovda, Molteni, Wu & Gomez-Pinilla
Found that, in rats, voluntary exercise can help recover function after traumatic brain injury.

2004
Will, Galani, Kelche & Rosenzweig
Corroborated earlier findings from animal studies that environmental enrichment and physical exercise increase neurogenesis in the hippocampus.

2004
Molteni, Wu, Vaynman, Ying, Barnard & Gomez-Pinilla
Unveiled a possible molecular mechanism by which lifestyle interacts with the brain—exercise reverses the harmful cognitive effects of a high-fat diet on brain plasticity in animals.

2004
Paul Adlard & Carl Cotman
Identified voluntary exercise as an intervention that can reverse central nervous system dysfunctions such as cognitive decline, depression, and stress.

2004
Vaynman, Ying & Gomez-Pinilla
Found that exercise enhances learning and memory in animals.

2005
Uysal, Tugyan, Kayatekin, Acikgoz, Bagriyanik, Gonenc, Ozdemir, et al.
Showed that exercise induced significant cognitive improvement throughout brain maturation in adolescent rats.

© Jean-Michel Cornet

Generating Energy and Maintaining Attention

Mr. Chin

Welcome to Las Vegas, Nevada, where summer tempera-
tures can reach 125 degrees during the day! At Lincoln
Elementary School, the regular school year lasts until June
18 and summer school is popular in the community.

Mr. Chin teaches summer school every year at Lincoln
because he loves teaching (and likes earning the extra
money). Still, it's a tough assignment. Keeping the students
on task and focused on the content is hard to do in the heat.
Kids are usually thinking about going swimming or to an air-
conditioned movie instead of sitting at school. Concentration
is very difficult when the entire class is sweaty and tired.

His six years of teaching experience have taught him well,
though. Mr. Chin relies heavily on energizers and attention
grabbers in academic classrooms, especially when his

students start zoning out. Approximately every ten or fifteen minutes, he plans something physical to do, even if it's a simple activity like standing up, walking five steps in any direction, and saying hello to the person you meet. These small movements not only gain students' attention, they keep him alert and focused, too.

Why Use Energizers?

Rather than snapping at students returning from lunch with glazed eyes, energize them! The icebreakers and energizers in this section of the book can be used at any point during any type of lesson in your academic classroom. If you tune students back into your lesson, the rest of the day will be more fun for everybody.

Kids are wired to move. Trying to keep still in a chair for seven hours a day can seem like a fool's errand. Think of it this way: How many times have you personally been in a lecture, meeting, or seminar that bored you stiff? It was easy to tune out the speaker because you had the grocery list, plans for the upcoming weekend, and other errands and adventures to think about instead. When you are afraid that the ZZZs are taking over your class, wake up the students with energizers!

Energizers are not throwaway activities randomly inserted into your schedule. They are purposeful interludes that you use strategically. There are three common times when students are likely to be de-energized and less willing to return to the classroom agenda:

1. After a meal
2. After recess
3. When a long lesson begins to drag

Using energizers can greatly enhance the impact of learning because they focus the learner on your lesson and raise the energy level of the class. Simple energizers include having students jump in place at their desks and applauding themselves with a standing ovation to acknowledge a job well done. A list of more involved energizers is below.

Use energizers to:

✔ **Promote readiness for learning.** Students do not learn well when they have low energy. Sluggishness can lead to a lack of attentiveness, and the phenomenon can be contagious with a class. Slouching in chairs, leaning on desks, and other nonverbal behaviors can be subliminally observed and copied by other class members. Energizers ready students to engage in the lesson.

✔ **Create excitement.** You're excited about the content of your lesson but that does not mean that your students are equally stimulated. Energizers can generate a positive expectation of upcoming events.

✔ **Overcome the effects of fatigue, drowsiness, and drag.** Long days, hot rooms, difficult material—all these factors can put students into a mild stupor. Energizers can wake them up and refresh them for the rest of the class.

✔ **Develop a sense of shared fun.** You can facilitate even the most serious discussions with comic relief, as long as you keep a proper perspective on the state standards and the outcomes of the lesson. An occasional group laugh makes any lesson livelier.

Getting and Keeping Attention

Energizers and state changes are wonderful techniques to start a class or energize at any given moment. If done properly, such strategies create an enhanced learning environment; boost a sense of teamwork; and get students acquainted, talking, and involved. When you do decide to employ one, follow these guidelines for success:

- Be quick.
- Involve everyone.
- Ensure the reason for the activity is relevant and obvious.
- Adapt the activity to the age, interests, and comfort level of your class.
- Enjoy yourself.
- Thank students for participating.

After a while, the class will anticipate and expect these activities and you can experiment with the length, content, and different methods. Encourage students to bring new activities to class and even let them teach and lead their peers.

Got it? *Let's get energized!*

Sculptor and Stone

Materials Needed: None
Directions:
1. Put students into pairs. One person is the "Sculptor" and the other is the "Stone."
2. Have the "Sculptor" create a statue out of the "Stone" that is related in some way to the lesson.
3. When all of the statues are made, let the "Sculptors" take a gallery walk and look at all the statues.
4. Have students switch places and repeat the activity.

Data Processing

Materials Needed: None
Directions:
Have students, without talking, put themselves in order according to different criteria that you set (longest hair, oldest to youngest, number of letters in their full name, etc.).

Dancing in JELL-O®

Materials Needed: None
Directions:
Have students cross the room as if they were trying to move through gelatin (they would have to move slowly against quite a bit of resistance). Have them move independently or following a leader.

Partner Macarena

Materials Needed: The song "Macarena" by Los Del Rio
Directions:
1. Review the "Macarena" dance motions (or ask a student to demonstrate and teach it if you don't remember it).
2. Put students into pairs.
3. Play the Macarena music and have the pairs dance the Macarena facing each other.

31 Days

Materials Needed: None
Directions:
1. Have students make a fist.
2. Tell them they are going to count off the months of the year on their knuckles.
3. Start at the pinky knuckle with January, move into the valley for February, the ring finger knuckle for March, and so on. When they hit the index finger knuckle with July, they start over on that knuckle for August and then reverse direction to finish the year.
4. Point out that months landing on a knuckle have 31 days in them. The months landing in a valley have 30 (except February).

Hand Jive

Materials Needed: The song "Hand Jive" by Johnny Otis (or another artist)
Directions:
1. Review the "Hand Jive" motions (or ask a student to demonstrate and teach it if you don't remember it).
2. Play the music.
3. Have students stand up at their desks and do the Hand Jive with the song.

Freeze Frame

Materials Needed: The song "The Twist" by Chubby Checker (or another artist)
Directions:
1. Review the motions of "The Twist" (or ask a student to demonstrate and teach it if you don't remember it).
2. Play the music.
3. Have students stand up at their desks and do the Twist with the song.
4. At randomly spaced intervals, stop the music and tell students to freeze in place. Have them look around the room and enjoy their classmates' silly postures.

One Behind

Materials Needed: None
Directions:
1. Ask a student volunteer to be the leader.
2. The leader comes to the front of the room and demonstrates a movement (for example, putting the hands on the hips).

3. The rest of the class performs the same movement.
4. The leader performs a second movement (for example, putting the hands on the knees).
5. The rest of the class performs the first movement.
6. The leader performs a third movement.
7. The rest of the class performs the second movement—always one behind!
8. Choose a different leader after several movements.

Chair Dance

Materials Needed: Chairs, upbeat music
Directions:
Have students sit in their chairs. Play music and have them dance while sitting—the more outrageous the moves, the better! If the class needs inspiration, have a volunteer lead the dance from the front of the room.

Paper Plate Dance

Materials Needed: Two paper plates per student, upbeat music

Directions:
1. Distribute the paper plates to the students.
2. Play the music.
3. Have students dance in place while standing at their seats, waving, tossing, fanning, and moving the plates in any creative way they can think of.

Ball Toss

Materials Needed: Several balls or pieces of crumpled paper for throwing safely inside a classroom
Directions:
1. Put students in one big circle or separate the class into three or four smaller circles.
2. Distribute one or two balls to each circle.
3. One student tosses the ball while asking a review question; the student who catches it answers the question.
4. When students are good at throwing and catching the balls within the confines of the circle, have the groups use other balls at the same time, creating patterns as they throw and answer.

I Like People Who...

Materials Needed: None
Directions:
1. Have students spread out in an open area or stand next to their seats.
2. Begin a sentence with the words, "I like people who...," and complete the sentence with a desired behavior for the class.
3. Have the students repeat the sentence and act out the behavior.
4. As a student volunteer to lead a few rounds.

Have You Ever?

Materials Needed: None
Directions:
1. Have students stand in a large circle, with a student volunteer in the middle.
2. The student in the middle asks the group a question that begins, "Have you ever...?" Possible ways to finish the question are, "...traveled to Alaska?" "...run a 5K race?" "...made the bed for your sister?"
3. Students who can answer yes to the question run to switch places. The student in the center also runs to fill one of the vacant spots.
4. Whoever is left without a space in the circle goes to the middle and asks the next question.

Reflex

Materials Needed: One table and one ball of crumpled paper for every eight students
Directions:
1. Break students into groups of four. Each student within a group is assigned the number 1, 2, 3, or 4.
2. Send two groups to each table and have them stand on opposite sides.
3. Place one crumpled ball of paper on the center of each table.
4. Tell students that you are going to call out a number from 1 to 4. Students with that number should try to grab the ball of paper. The team of the student who grabs the ball gets a point.

No Hands

Materials Needed: Objects of various shapes and sizes
Directions:
Scatter the objects around the room and have students take turns picking up and carrying the objects across the room—without using their hands.

Limbo

Materials Needed: Long jump ropes or poles, upbeat music
Directions:
1. Break the class into three or four groups.
2. Give each group a jump rope or pole to use as a limbo stick.
3. Have two students hold the limbo stick with one side higher than the other so students can decide how low they want to go.
4. Play music and have students walk under the limbo stick. Periodically stop the music and have two students switch with the stick holders so everyone gets a turn to play.

Clapping Games

Materials Needed: None
Directions:
Have students take turns inventing and performing clapping rhythms and patterns. Experiment with teams and creating games out of the activity.

Penny Pass

Materials Needed: Pennies
Directions:
1. Divide the students into groups of six. Spread them out so that each group of six faces another group of six.
2. Give a penny to each group.
3. At your signal, students try to pass the penny to their teammates while disguising their progress from the other team.
4. When you call "stop," the teams try to guess who has the penny on the other team.

Lap Sit

Materials Needed: None
Directions:
1. Have students stand shoulder to shoulder in as tight a circle as possible.
2. Tell everyone to turn to the left (to face clockwise) and then shuffle towards the center until they are standing in an even tighter signal.
3. At your signal, tell everyone to carefully sit down in the lap of the person behind them.
4. At your next signal, have everyone carefully stand up.
5. Turn students in the opposite direction for another lap sit.

Switch Something

Materials Needed: None
Directions:
1. Put students into pairs and have them stand facing their partners.
2. At your signal, tell students to turn their backs on their partners and change three things about themselves.
3. At your next signal, the partners face each other and try to figure out what has changed.

1 to 20

Materials Needed: None
Directions:
1. Divide the students into groups of six.
2. Have the groups stand shoulder to shoulder in a tight circle and bow their heads to look at the floor.
3. Without making eye contact, students in the group try to count—one person at a time—from 1 to 20. If two people say a number at the same time, the group must start over from 1.

Psychic Shake

Materials Needed: Upbeat music
Directions:
1. Tell students to silently choose a number from 1 to 3 and to keep it a secret.
2. Start playing the music. When the music starts, students walk around the room, shaking hands with the people they meet, according to the numbers they have secretly chosen and without revealing their numbers in any way. For example, a person who has chosen the number 1 would give one shake of the hand; a person who has chosen number 3 would shake three times.
3. If two people who have chosen the same number shake hands and discover each other, they link arms and continue looking for other people to shake hands with.
4. Keep playing until students have found everyone with like numbers and there are three big groups with linked arms.

Aura

Materials Needed: None
Directions:
1. Put students into pairs and have them stand facing their partners at arm's length.
2. Tell students to touch their palms together and close their eyes.
3. At your signal, partners drop their palms, turn around three times, and try to touch palms again—still with their eyes closed.

Shoulder Circles

Materials Needed: None
Directions:
1. Have students stand shoulder to shoulder in a tight circle and turn to the left (face clockwise).
2. At your signal, tell them to put both hands on the shoulders of the person in front of them. Try to make this a simultaneous movement.
3. Using the heel of the hand or the thumb, students make circles on the right shoulder and shoulder blade of the person in front of them. After a few moments, have them make circles on the left shoulder and shoulder blade, then use both hands to make circles on both shoulders.
4. Finally, tell students to doodle on the back of the person in front of them, making figure eights or spelling words, covering the whole space from top to bottom.

Depending on your group, you may want to briefly discuss the issues of boundaries and respect before beginning this activity.

Power Walk

Materials Needed: None (stopwatch optional)
Directions:
Challenge your students to see if they can walk as fast as you can! If you are using a stopwatch, have students calculate their heart rates before and after the activity, and discuss the differences.

Quick-n-Easy Energizers

Materials Needed: None
Directions:
- Tell jokes
- Do a line dance (like the Electric Slide)
- Stretch or perform a yoga posture
- Keep a beach ball in the air for two minutes
- Have students invent wacky handshakes
- Play a round of duck-duck-goose
- Have thumb-wrestling matches
- Play a round of musical chairs (but have enough chairs for everyone)
- Play toe-tac-tic (the object is to force your partner to win)
- Play Simon Says
- Tell tongue twisters

State Changes

When learning new material, students are bombarded with masses of sensory data. Somehow teachers must make learning goals stand out in their pupils' minds, even as their brains are uploading all kinds of new information. State changes—stimulus that brings about a change in a student's thoughts, feelings, or physiology—are an effective technique for highlighting what needs to be of focus (Allen, 2001). When teachers combine repetition of material with state changes, student recall and comprehension increases.

Some basic state changes include substituting novelty for a class ritual or process once in a while, changing the tone or volume of your voice, leaving provocative sentences unfinished (maybe even at the end of the day!), and playing a song during a transition and asking students to guess its significance to the lesson.

Directional State Changes

Materials Needed: None
Directions:
Redirect student attention with the words you say. Try the following sentences during your next lesson:

- "Turn to your neighbor and say..." (hello, a math fact, your homework assignment)
- "Raise your hand if..." (you feel ready for tomorrow's test, you remember something from last week's lesson, you have new information about this topic)
- "Please look at the poster for..." (Refer to a visual display in the classroom.)
- "May I have all eyes at the front of the room?"
- "Please turn your chairs to face me."
- "If you agree, put your thumbs up. If you disagree, put your thumbs down."
- "Everyone take a deep breath. Now, if you agree [with the issue at hand], exhale."
- "Clap and cheer if you are ready to learn!"
- "Turn to someone close to you and say, 'yes!'"

Traveling State Changes

Materials Needed: None
Directions:
Put students in motion to change their state (and ignite their curiosity).

- Have students switch seats without warning.
- Have students take seven steps in any direction and sit down.
- Have students touch two walls in the classroom and then return to their seats.
- Have students touch something in the room that is green and return to their seats.
- Have students crawl under the nearest table and find a new seat.
- Have students shake the hands of three people who... (Fill in a personal detail—people who have a younger brother, for example—to complete the sentence.)

Question State Changes

Materials Needed: None
Directions:
Ask silly questions and have students raise their hands if they fit the description. Start your questions with the phrase, "Who...?" Use students, celebrities, and yourself as points of comparison.

- ...is wearing the same color shoes as...
- ...has a birthday in the same month as...
- ...shares a middle initial with...
- ...plays the same sport as...
- ...lives closest to...
- ...has the longest hair

Tossing Objects State Changes

Materials Needed: Various
Directions:

- Toss out candy to students who answer questions (make sure everyone gets to answer one).
- Toss your pen or chalkboard eraser in the air as a surprise.
- Instead of distributing handouts, walk to the center of the room and toss them into the air for students to gather.
- Have students toss each other a foam ball or crumpled sheet of newspaper as they take turns answering questions.

Integrating Movement and Academics

Ms. Millstone

When it comes to teaching first grade, they don't make teachers any more qualified or successful than Ms. Millstone. Although she has only been teaching for two years, you wouldn't guess it. Her demeanor, rapport, and communication skills with children are phenomenal.

Teaching at Oakville Elementary School in Columbus, Ohio, is a treat in itself, and not just because it is a brand-new school in a very safe area. There's another upside—she's a born educator. On the other hand, her charisma and talent have created some tensions and garnered jealousy from a few veteran teachers on staff.

Why would some experienced teachers feel threatened by a new teacher like Ms. Millstone? Well, the kids love her class and all she seems to do is play games with them. More than one teacher in the faculty lounge has ominously said,

"We'll just see what happens when the state testing scores come in. I'm sure playtime will stop then!"

Little do they realize, however, that Ms. Millstone is very knowledgeable about how children learn. Her motto is, "Students are there to learn, not to hear me to teach." And indeed, her students are the most engaged and enthusiastic in the school. When the standardized test scores come in at the end of the year, she has no doubt they'll be stellar.

True Learning

Reflect on this scenario. Do the teachers at your school keep up with what the research says about how we as humans really learn? Do you? Because you made the decision to read this far into the book, you are probably now a lot more aware than most educators are about using physical movement to improve student achievement and learning—and your students are now in a position to have a lot more fun!

Aligning movement and academic concepts is essential for true learning to occur. The integration of content-area information with movement can often be accomplished with minimal effort and maximum benefit. And the benefit is twofold because children don't just increase learning of physical activities and academic knowledge, they also come to recognize interconnectedness between physical activity and how it applies to all areas of their lives. Anchoring of the learning through procedural learning—the act of doing instead of being a spectator—increases the learning of the content exponentially.

The Learning Hierarchy

Learning academic subject matter through different modalities will only reinforce the content in multiple mediums. The hierarchy of learning explains this well. In a traditional classroom, the usual routine is one in which children read, hear what the teacher has to say, and see what is on the board. Unfortunately, we tend to retain only half of what we see and hear. But as you climb the learning pyramid, you can see that the more engaged the learner, the more learning occurs.

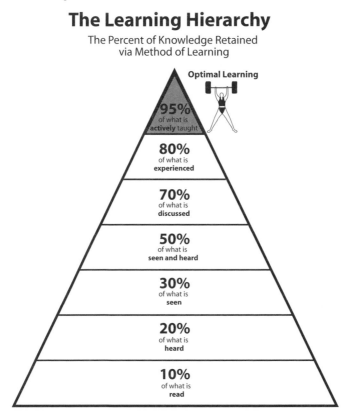

The Learning Hierarchy

The Percent of Knowledge Retained
via Method of Learning

Optimal Learning

95%
of what is
actively taught

80%
of what is
experienced

70%
of what is
discussed

50%
of what is
seen and heard

30%
of what is
seen

20%
of what is
heard

10%
of what is
read

Instructional methods should offer high contrast, alternating between repetitive, sedentary activities and active lessons. Instruction should include more visually stimulating, interactive, diverse material. Students need to be taught that there are learning preferences as well as differences in the way their brains receive, process, and express information. Subjects that traditionally and solely use linguistically based content instruction should try to incorporate more movement, music, and action into their instruction. Stimulating, engaging instruction should be given increased priority in the school day!

Movement Facilitates Cognition

Carefully consider these questions as you add more movement to the curriculum.

- What are you teaching?
- Who are you teaching?
- Are your students learning the material being taught?

When adding more action, most of the time teachers do not need to reinvent the wheel. You already have a wealth of information and tools that you are using and doing. Ask yourself, then, how you can add to what you are already doing. Assess your strengths and build on them. You're already skilled at teaching—just expand your style.

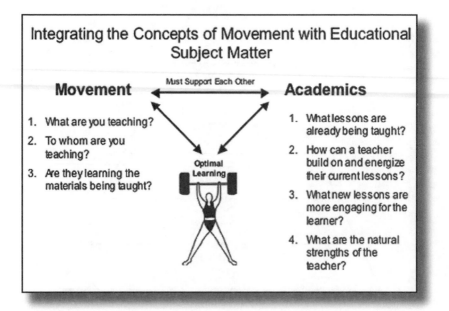

Academic Movement Reminders

The following activities can provide much-needed action to various academic subject matters—Math, Language Arts, Science, Social Studies, Health, and P.E. As you read through and select activities to try, keep the following considerations in mind:

Age Level

Although these activities are designed for a broad range of ages, you still should consider what would work with your students. Consider, for example, the activity, *Phonics Phitness*. Phonics is often considered early elementary material but you may teach upper elementary. Use the game as a template by taking the basic guidelines and adjusting to the material you are teaching. Don't throw out an idea before first trying to adapt it. You might be surprised by what your class likes the most.

Equipment

Don't toss out a game because you don't have the specific equipment it calls for. The activities are, in most cases, flexible enough to use ordinary objects you may already have on hand. Don't have poly spots? Use paper plates. Remember, though, that substitutions may require you to make extra safety precautions. Poly spots stick to the ground by design; paper plates slide around—and a kid who jumps aggressively onto one may slide with it! Think safety first. (Hint: To keep paper plates from sliding, stick rubber grippers to the bottom of them before using them in an activity.)

Creativity

Be creative with the rules, set–up, and content of the game. You are the one that makes the rules in the end.

Facilities

Every school is different. If you don't have a big classroom, swap for an afternoon with another teacher who does, take advantage of a multi-purpose room or gymnasium, or go outside. Adapt! Where there's a will, there's a way.

Flexibility

The main objective is to get your students engaged in active learning. Don't worry if an activity does not go perfectly. The kids probably won't know the difference between what they are doing and what is written in the book. They're just happy they get to move.

Music

Whenever possible, include music. Music is a very powerful draw into any activity and adds a sense of festivity. Besides, you can find music that matches just about any subject matter activity. Do whatever you can to reinforce the academic content with sounds or lyrics.

Now, get moving! (And enjoy...)

Action-Packed Mathematics

Hundreds Chart

Purpose: Reinforce mental math strategies
Materials Needed: Hundreds chart for each student

Directions:
1. Pass out a hundreds chart to each student.
2. Direct students to put their fingers on a specific number—without talking—by giving them a cue. For example, the first cue might be, "How many sides does a triangle have?" The second cue might be, "Square that number." The third cue might be, "Multiply that number by 7."
3. After about the tenth cue, ask student volunteers to announce what number they have.
4. Reveal the correct number.
5. Announce, "Change seats!" and have students take their hundreds chart to another spot in the room.
6. Play upbeat, exciting music during the transition; when the music stops, have students take a seat for another round of cues.

Hundreds Chart

1	11	21	31	41	51	61	71	81	91
2	12	22	32	42	52	62	72	82	92
3	13	23	33	43	53	63	73	83	93
4	14	24	34	44	54	64	74	84	94
5	15	25	35	45	55	65	75	85	95
6	16	26	36	46	56	66	76	86	96
7	17	27	37	47	57	67	77	87	97
8	18	28	38	48	58	68	78	88	98
9	19	29	39	49	59	69	79	89	99
10	20	30	40	50	60	70	80	90	100

Math Mayhem

Purpose: Practice simple math computations

Materials Needed: One pair of dice per each group of four students

Directions:
1. Break students into groups of four.
2. Direct one person in each group to throw the dice in a certain way (for example, underhand, overhand, with their right hand, left hand, etc.).
3. Students add up the numbers shown on the dice and form the total number using their bodies.
4. Have students take turns throwing the dice within the group.
5. After a few minutes have passed, ask students to form new groups of four.

Variations:
- Add restrictions to how students can form the numbers with their bodies. For example, say that they can use only their arms or only the left side of the body.
- Have students subtract, multiply, or divide the numbers on the dice.
- Have students demonstrate answers with hops, jumping jacks, or other physical movements.
- Have a group of students use their bodies to represent an entire math problem with their bodies for another group to solve and display with their bodies.

Olympic Math

Purpose: Reinforce the order of operations
Materials Needed: A pencil and sheet of paper for each student; a pair of dice and a deck of cards for every two students

Directions:
1. Ask students to take out a sheet of paper and a pencil.
2. Put students into pairs.
3. Give each pair of students a deck of cards and pair of dice.
4. Students shuffle the deck and deal out sixteen cardsface up in a 4 x 4 array.
5. The first student rolls the dice. The sum of the dice becomes the target number. (For example, a roll of 6 and 3 would result in the target number 9.) The second student takes the first turn.
6. A turn consists of using the order of operations to combine cards from the array to reach the target number. Cards equal their face value. Aces count as 1; jacks, queens, and kings count as 10. A student may not combine more than five cards in one turn. Players keep the cards they have used in their hand.
7. Players take turns combining cards until there are no more cards in the array or until no combination results in the target number.
8. Players add up the value of cards in their hand; the player with the highest number wins the round.
9. Set the cards aside and deal another array with the cards left in the deck.
10. Play another round until all the cards in the deck have been used.

Variation:
Have students multiply the numbers on the dice for the target number.

Jumpin' & Hoppin' Hoops

Purpose: Reinforce basic math skills
Materials Needed: 6–10 hula hoops per group of eight students and foam dice

Directions:
1. Break students into groups of eight.
2. For each group, arrange a set of hula hoops on the floor so that they are all touching (creating a path of hula hoops).
3. Roll the dice and ask a student volunteer to total the number.
4. As a class, determine if the number is odd or even.
4. If the number is odd, have students hop on one foot through each hula hoop in the path as fast as they can. If the number is even, have students jump with both feet through each hula hoop.

Variation:
Change the way students travel through the hula hoops. For example, have them gallop with odd numbers and skip with even numbers.

Jumping Numbers

Purpose: Practice addition and subtraction skills
Materials Needed: One jump rope per student, and lots of open space

Directions:
1. Distribute a jump rope to each student.
2. Ask students to spread out so they can jump without bumping into each other.
3. Call out a math problem appropriate to your class's skill level.
4. Have students call out the answer in chorus and then jump the rope until they reach that number, counting aloud as they go.

Variation:
Add other directions to how they jump the rope, such as backwards, with crossed arms, or on one foot.

Multiples in Motion

Purpose: Practice multiples of the numbers 1 through 9
Materials Needed: Balls/paper wads/objects of different sizes, shapes, and weight

Directions:
1. Begin the activity by demonstrating multiples of 1 and 2 to the entire class.
   For multiples of 1, count aloud and clap your hands once as you say each multiple of 1 (you would clap for every number). Demonstrate up to the number 10. For multiples of 2, clap without counting aloud, but snap and say the number when you reach a multiple of 2. The pattern would be (silence)/clap, "two"/snap, (silence)/clap, "four"/snap, (silence)/clap, "six"/snap, et cetera.
2. As a group, have students practice the multiples of 2 up to the number 20.
3. Put students into groups of three or four.
4. Assign to each group a number from 3 to 9.
5. Tell groups that they have to design and practice a sequence for the multiples of their number. For example, a group assigned the number 4 would have a four-motion sequence, perhaps (silence)/clap, (silence)/snap, (silence)/stomp, "four"/jump, silence)/clap, (silence)/snap, (silence)/stomp, "eight"/jump, et cetera.
6. Call all the groups together after about fifteen minutes and have them perform their moving multiples for the rest of the class.

Variation:
Allow students to use props, like a bouncing ball or a scarf, during their sequences.

Human Number Line

Purpose: Practice sequencing positive and negative numbers
Materials Needed: Number card for each student

Preparation:
To play this game, your class will be separated into two teams, so create two sets of number cards (two different colors of index cards work well for this). You will need to make a card for each student.

Each set of cards will represent the same range of positive and negative numbers. For example, if you have thirty students in your class, each team will have fifteen people on it; in each set of number cards, you would make a card for the numbers −7 to +7 (including 0). If you have If you had fourteen students on a team, you might use the numbers from −6 to +7. Write one number on each card, large enough so that it would be readable to a person standing several feet away.

If one team is short one person, just remove the largest or smallest number from that team's set of number cards.

Directions:
1. Conduct a class review of the number line, emphasizing the left-to-right order of smaller to greater numbers and the relationships of positive and negative numbers to zero.
2. Break the class into two teams and have them stand arms' length apart in two facing lines.
3. Quickly review again the left-right/smaller-greater order of numbers, asking students to raise and wave their left arms and right arms for emphasis.
4. Pass out, in random order, the sets of number cards to each team.
5. Tell students that they will move around the room to music. When the music stops, they are to reassemble themselves in number line order.
5. Play music and direct students to move around the room in a silly way (giant steps in any direction, galloping like a horse, hopping backwards, et cetera).
6. When the music stops, have the teams form their number lines, each student holding their card above their head so you and the opposite team can see it.
7. The team who correctly reforms the number line first scores a point.
8. Have students exchange cards with their teammates and play another round.
9. Play to five points and declare one team the winner!

Variation:
Make a third set of larger number cards for yourself (overhead transparencies work well for this). Display one of the numbers and have teams form the number with their bodies while standing (the entire team makes one number). When one team has made the number, call out "number line!" Both teams then race to arrange themselves in order as before. Award a point to the team that makes the number first and a point to the team that makes the number line first.

Recipes for Success

Purpose: Apply math skills to real life problems

Materials Needed: Recipes, pictures of the ingredients labeled with their prices, jump ropes (optional), pencils and scratch paper, desks or tables for activity stations, tasty rewards

Preparation:
Set up at least one of each of the following stations. Spread them out as far as you can.

- Recipe Box—Have enough copies of a recipe for each student pair. If you wish, you may provide several different recipes for students to choose from. Also have paper available so students can write down ingredients and prices, and make calculations.
- Grocery Store—Display pictures of every ingredient for every recipe labeled with quantity and price (a bulletin board would work well for this). Or, you could have enough labeled pictures of each ingredient so students could collect them from a large table.
- Checkout Lane—Ensure that there is enough space for students to sit and total their purchases.
- Kitchen—You will need work space for every pair of students. At the workspace, provide a jump rope, two "division" sheets, and two "multiplication" sheets.
- Manager's Office—Set up a place for students to come to you to share their completed work or ask questions. Have treats on hand to give to students when they complete their work. (If possible, have treats that match the recipes you use in this activity.)

Directions:
1. Assign students into pairs.
2. Send each pair to the Recipe Box to select a recipe and get a sheet of paper.
3. Have student pairs run from the Recipe Box to the Grocery Store.
4. Students "shop" at the grocery store by collecting the items they need for the recipe or writing down their quantities and cost on the sheet of paper.
5. Students jump to the Checkout Lane and total the cost of their groceries.
6. Students skip to the Kitchen and find a workspace.
7. Have one student cut the recipe in half and recalculate the cost on the "division" sheet while the other jumps rope. (If you do not have jump ropes, have the student do jumping jacks.) When the first student is finished, the partners switch places.
8. Have one student double the recipe and recalculate the cost on the "multiplication" sheet while the other jumps rope (or does jumping jacks). Again, switch places.

9. When the students have finished in the Kitchen, they bring their work to Manager's Office for approval. Have them jog in place as you check their work.
10. If the students have completed their recipe correctly, reward them with a treat! If they have not, send them back to the Kitchen to try again.

Place Value Taggers

Purpose: Practice place value from the ones to the millions place
Materials Needed: Identification badges (or jerseys, hats, colored buttons, etc.), index cards with various numbers (three to seven digits long) written on them, open space for a game of tag

Directions:
1. Assign the role of "Card Holder" to a quarter of your students and give them an identifying badge (or jersey, hat, colored button, etc) and card with a number on it.
2. Assign the role of "Tagger" to the rest of the students.
3. Tell students that when the music starts, Taggers will move around according to your directions, trying to tag each other. Card Holders are exempt from tagging. Students who are tagged must freeze in place.
4. Card Holders approach the frozen Taggers and point to a digit in the number on the cards that they have. The frozen Tagger must name the place value of that digit correctly in order to return to the game.
5. After about a minute, stop the music and have Card Holders give their cards and identifying badge to a Tagger for another round of play.

Measuring Up

Purpose: Practice estimation skills
Materials Needed: 1 length of rope, a hoop, a ruler, and pencil and paper for each student (ropes and hoops should be of varying sizes)

Directions:
1. Conduct a review of inches, feet, and yards.
2. Distribute a length of rope to each student. Ask students to arrange the ropes in straight lines.
3. Have students balance and walk across the rope, measuring its length according to their own foot length. If they fall off the rope they must begin again.
4. Have students walk on top of the hoop to measure its circumference in "feet."
5. Have students compare the length of the rope to the circumference of the hoop in "feet."

6. Have students locate someone else's hoop with a circumference that is the same as the length of their own rope.
7. Have students use the ruler to measure and record the actual length of the rope and circumference of their hoop in inches, feet, and yards.

Variations:
- Direct students to balance and walk on the ropes and hoops in different ways—on their toes, sideways, backwards, as fast as possible, et cetera.
- Practice other math skills. For example, have students find a rope that is twice as long as the circumference of their hoop.

Clockwise Craziness

Purpose: Review the concepts of clockwise and counterclockwise
Materials Needed: 12 paper plates with the numbers 1 to 12 written on them; two yardsticks, pointers, or baseball bats; large open play space

Directions:
1. Conduct a quick review of clockwise and counterclockwise with the class.
2. Arrange the numbers 1 through 12 in a large circle to represent a clock face. Place the yardsticks at the center of the circle like clock hands as a point of reference.
3. Have students spread themselves out around the clock face.
4. Tell students to move (skip, hop, walk fast, grapevine, etc.) in either a clockwise or counterclockwise direction until the music stops.
5. After a few moments, stop the music and give different movement directions. For example, if students were skipping clockwise, you might now have them gallop counterclockwise. Note: Alternating predictably between clockwise and counterclockwise will make the game too easy.
6. Stop and start the music until the students are comfortable with the difference between clockwise and counterclockwise.

Variation:
Apply the math skills of addition and subtraction to the clock to practice past and future times.

Math Circuits

Purpose: Review basic math skills

Materials Needed: Index cards with basic math computation questions written on them (for example, "2 x 3 = ?" or "5 + 7 = ?")—five for each station; a variety of sporting equipment, depending on the stations you set up; a large, open area

Directions:

1. Set up as many stations as you can, depending on space and equipment available. The following is a list of ten station ideas; use your imagination!
   - Jump ropes
   - Hula hoops
   - Throwing bean bags onto a floor target
   - Paddles with balls attached by rubber strings
   - Tossing Koosh® balls underhand into a bucket or trash can
   - Dribbling a basketball
   - Kicking a foam ball at a wall
   - Tossing and catching a Koosh® ball with a partner
   - Keeping a beach ball in the air
   - Volleying a balloon with knees, elbows, or your head

2. Place five index cards upside down in a pile at each station.
3. Break students into pairs and assign each pair to a station. If there are more pairs than stations, place some pairs between stations and have them jog or hop in place while reciting math facts until a station is free.
4. At each station, students alternate turning over an index card, solving the math problem, and acting out the answer with the sports equipment. For example, if the answer to a problem is 4, the student would jump rope four times or dribble a basketball four times (depending on the station).
5. Students return the index card to the bottom of the pile after solving the problem.
6. When enough time has passed for each partner to have one or two turns at the station, rotate the student pairs to the next station.

Action-Packed Language Arts

Acrostics

Purpose: Reinforce spelling and vocabulary words
Materials Needed: Paper, pencils, colored markers, crayons, etc.

Directions:
1. Distribute paper and writing utensils to each student.
2. Have students write their names vertically down the left side of the paper. Encourage them to use different colors and to be creative.
3. Have students spell out their names with their bodies, letter by letter.
4. Then, for each letter of their name, have students identify a spelling or vocabulary word from class that starts with the same letter. Write and illustrate these words next to the appropriate letters.

Loco Moves

Purpose: Understand the differences between verbs and adverbs
Materials Needed: Index card for each student—half the cards should have a movement verb written on them (i.e., skip, hop, slide) and the other half should have adverbs (i.e., quietly, rapidly, quickly); one bean bag per student

Directions:
1. Distribute the bean bags to the students.
2. Have students find their own personal space in an open area.
3. Spread out the index cards face up on the floor in the same area that the students are standing.
4. Have students toss their bean bags in a specified manner (underhand, with your non-dominant hand, high in the air) toward an index card. Each student should aim at a different card—help them coordinate this.
5. Instruct students to move in a specified manner (backwards, hopping) to pick up the cards their bean bags landed on.
6. Students must determine if the word on the card is a verb or an adverb. Students with adverbs should hold the cards high above their heads and find a student with a verb card.
7. Both students in an adverb–verb pair perform the action on the verb card in the manner specified by the adverb card: skip quickly, laugh loudly, etc.
8. Once students have performed the actions, they place their cards back on the floor, retrieve a bean bag, find a personal space, and toss again, this time aiming at a different verb or adverb.

Word Shoot-Out

Purpose: Practice and reinforce spelling skills

Materials Needed: 6–8 basketball shooting stations, one basketball per station, poly spots/paper plates marked with letters, list of appropriate spelling words. Remember, modify regular balls and buckets if you don't have basketball courts.

Preparation:
1. Write one letter on each paper plate or poly spot. Have enough different letters at each station for students to be able to spell out multiple words with them. Remember that letters will be picked up as they are used to spell a word.
2. If you do not have access to basketball courts, set up stations with buckets or trash cans and Koosh balls or tightly wadded newspaper. Clearly delineate the boundaries of the station so students know what bucket to aim at.
3. Arrange the letters at random within the three-point line on a basketball court or within the delineated shooting area of a station.

Directions:
1. Split students into groups of three and send them to a station. Assign one student to the role of "Shooter," one to the role of "Runner," and the third to the role of "Rebounder."
2. Call out a spelling word. The Shooters at each station spell out the word by going to the letters and throwing the ball into the basket from that spot. When the shooter makes a basket, the Runner picks up that letter and places it on the baseline in spelling word order. The Rebounder collects the ball from missed shots and returns it to the shooter.
3. When a group decides that the word is spelled correctly, they sit on the ground and do toe touches and stretches as they wait for the teacher to check their word.
4. The group that first sits down and has spelled the word correctly gets to choose the next word.
5. Students switch roles with every word—the Runner becomes the next Shooter, the Shooter the Rebounder, and the Rebounder the Runner.

Scrabble Scramble

Purpose: Increase vocabulary knowledge
Materials Needed: One piece of paper and pencil per group; one set of index cards that reflect the distribution of letters as a Scrabble set (nine letter As, two letter Bs, twelve letter Es, four letter Ts, etc.) per group; large, open space

Directions:
1. Divide the class into groups of two or three. (Students in groups larger than this will not receive the same cardiovascular benefits.)
2. Distribute the sets of index cards to each student group and ask them to shuffle the set thoroughly.
3. Divide the playing area in half. Send the all the groups to one half of the area and have them spread out their cards face up. Make sure that the groups' cards don't run into each other.
4. Bring the students back to the other half of the playing area.
5. On your signal and one group member at a time, students hop, skip, or jump (you provide the movement instructions) to their cards, pick one up, and bring it back to the group.
6. When a group has enough cards to spell a word, they bring their word to the teacher for verification. Groups must record all their verified words on their papers.
7. Students take turns collecting letters until you call time.
8. Award words of four letters or less one point per word; award words of five letters or more two points per word.
9. Total the points per group and for the entire class, and celebrate success!

Body Language

Purpose: Practice spelling words
Materials Needed: Lines on the playing area floor, paper and pencil for each group

Directions:
1. Divide students into groups of three and send each group to their own section of a line.
2. Distribute the paper and pencils to each group.
3. Have the groups write down five two-letter words on their papers.
4. Once they have written their two-letter words, students must represent their words using their bodies. They must spell the word correctly and you must be able to read the word from left to right on the line.
5. Move through the student groups, reading and verifying the student body words.
6. Once a group has spelled out all five two-letter words, have them think of three-letter words to create.
7. The group that has spelled the most correct words when you call time wins!

Variations:
- Combine groups to enable them to spell longer words.
- Restrict what parts of their bodies the students can use to spell word
- Incorporate this activity into a lesson about shapes or another content-area skill.

Phonics Phitness

Purpose: Practice phonics
Materials Needed: Three sets of 26 paper plates or poly spots with one letter written on each plate

Directions:
1. Scatter the three sets of paper plates across the room.
2. Divide the class into groups of three or four students.
3. Call out a phonics question and direct students to move to the right letter in a certain way. For example, you might say, "Hop on one foot to the letter that makes the "huh" sound in "house." (Remind students that each letter appears in the room several times.)
4. Try to use each letter at least once during the activity.

Alphabet Tag

Purpose: Practice letter recognition
Materials Needed: Large, open, safe playing area with clearly marked boundaries

Directions:
1. Have students spread out in the playing area.
2. Assign one-third of the students to the role of Runner and the rest of them to the role of Tagger. Taggers tag each other; Runners are exempt from being tagged.
3. Students who are tagged must freeze in place and form a letter with their bodies. Before they can be unfrozen, a Runner must come up to them and correctly guess the letter that the student has made. Students may not be tagged during the guessing process.
4. Once the letter is guessed, the student is free to run and tag other students again. Students must form a different letter every time they are tagged.
5. After a few minutes, have the Runners switch places with Taggers so every student has a chance to form letters.

Sentence Detectives

Purpose: Identify parts of a sentence
Materials Needed: Index cards with different nouns, verbs, adjectives, and adverbs that can be combined to make complete sentences.

Preparation:
Choose action verbs that the students can perform as a group (i.e., twist, jump, bend) and adverbs that describe those verbs; choose nouns that can be easily located in the classroom and adjectives that describe those nouns. Create enough words so that several groups playing at one time can easily form sentences.

Directions:
1. Shuffle and spread out the cards face down in a specified section within the playing area (to one side or the middle).
2. Break students into groups of two or three and have the groups find space to sit in across from the cards. Groups should all be equidistant from the cards. (You may want to mark the groups' spots with a cone or other object.)
3. At your signal, and one group member at a time, students will crabwalk, crawl, or hop (you provide the movement instructions) to the cards, pick one up, and bring it back to the group. The student with the card tags the next teammate to go.
4. Groups continue retrieving cards until they have collected one noun, one verb, and one adverb. If a student brings back a card with a part of speech that the group already has, the next teammate in line decides which of the two cards to keep, and returns the extra to the pile of cards before selecting a new card.
5. Once a group has a sentence, the students stand up, call out, "Word play!" and then perform the action of the sentence.
6. When you call time, have the groups one by one read their sentence aloud, perform the action of the sentence for the rest of the class, and identify the part of speech of each word in the sentence.

Vowel Snatcher

Purpose: Identify vowel sounds
Materials Needed: A large, open, safe playing area with clearly marked boundaries and lines drawn (or taped) across both ends; identifying badges (hats, jerseys, name tags, or soft, visible objects to hold) for at least half the class

Directions:
1. Divide your class into two groups. Have one group stand on the line at one end of the playing area and the other group stand on the line at the other end.

2. Select two students—one from each group—and give them the role of "Tagger," as well as identifying badges.
3. Assign every other student to a vowel.
4. Call out a word and a specified movement (hopping, running, skipping, etc.).
5. Students assigned a vowel that is part of that word move across the room to the other line in the manner specified, trying to avoid being tagged. The Taggers, also moving in the manner specified, try to tag students as they cross the space. Any tagged students become Taggers themselves, and must get an identifying badge between rounds.

Variations:
• Present a list of the words used to the students after the activity and have them circle every instance of their personal vowels in the list.
• Assign consonants as well as, or instead of, vowels.

Absolutely Adverbs

Purpose: Reinforce the concept that adverbs describe verbs
Materials Needed: Large open space

Directions:
1. Review the rules of adverb usage with students, reminding them that most adverbs end in –ly.
2. Have students spread out in the open space.
3. Direct students to start moving in a certain way. For example, tell them to start walking.
4. Call out adverbs that describe different ways of moving. Students should modify their movements to reflect the adverb. For example, you could have them walk quickly, happily, secretly, or loudly.
5. Alter the specified movements and adverbs to give students lots of practice.

Action-Packed Science

Molecules in Motion

Purpose: Demonstrate the characteristics of molecules and the three states of matter

Materials Needed: Large open space and boundary markers

Directions:
1. Use the boundary markers to delineate a large space.
2. Assemble the entire class within the large space.
3. Announce that they are molecules and that molecules always move. Tell them they can move any way they want but that they can't touch one another.
4. Have the students move as quickly as they can for about one minute—without touching each other.
5. Stop them and decrease the space by about half. Tell them to move again—without touching.
6. Stop them and decrease the space until they are all in a very small area. Have them move as best they can, still without touching.
7. Sit the students down and explain that molecules that are far apart can move quickly and form gasses. As the area decreased, they were crowded closer together and had to move more slowly, like a liquid. When molecules are so close together that they can hardly move at all, they form a solid. Discuss their observations of the activity in relationship to what they just learned.

The Caterpillar Song

Purpose: Reinforce the stages of a butterfly's metamorphosis
Materials Needed: None

Directions:
1. Sing verse one (the lyrics and tune are below). Sing it again and have the class sing verse one with you. Sing verse two. Have the class sing verse two with you. Sing verse three. Have the class sing verse three with you.
2. Demonstrate the motions for verse one (the motions are below). Have the class do the same. Demonstrate the motions for verse two. Have the class do the same. Demonstrate the motions for verse three. Have the class do the same.
3. Sing the entire song with motions a few times through. Have the students do it once by themselves.

I'm a Fuzzy Caterpillar
(to the tune of "Mary Had a Little Lamb")

I'm a fuzzy caterpillar
caterpillar
caterpillar
I'm a fuzzy caterpillar about to make a cocoon.

I'm wrapped up in a cocoon
a cocoon
a cocoon
I'm wrapped up in a cocoon about to spread my wings.

I'm a pretty butterfly
butterfly
butterfly
I'm a pretty butterfly about to fly away.

Movements
First Verse: Hold out your left arm straight in front of you, and bend your elbow so your forearm is parallel to your chest. Use your right hand to imitate a caterpillar crawling along the ground (your left forearm).

Second Verse: Wrap your arms around yourself as if you were giving yourself a hug. Twist your torso right and left to add more motion.

Third Verse: Spread your arms out to your sides and flap them up and down as if you are flying.

Planet Hoop

Purpose: Review facts about different planets
Materials Needed: One hoop per student, a children's books about planets, "The Planets" music by Gustov Holst; an open space

Directions:
1. Distribute the hoops to the students. Have the students stand inside the hoops, holding the hoops up at their waist to make a "spaceship."
2. Tell students that they are going to fly their spaceships to visit different planets.
3. Instruct them to crouch with their hoops at the "launching pad" and jump up to "blast off" at your signal.
4. Count backwards from 5 to 0 and then yell "Blast off!"
5. Provide instructions for how students should move (hop, skip, walk, etc.) as they "fly" their "spaceships" around the room.
6. Play "The Planets" as students move around the room and fade it out when it is time to "land" on a planet.
7. Direct students to land by placing their hoop on the floor and sitting inside it. Once they are seated, use books and pictures to share two or three facts about the planet they are "visiting."
8. "Blast off" again.
9. After visiting four or five planets, have students travel back to Earth. Lead a discussion about how Earth is different from other planets.

Pedometer Prowlers

Purpose: Review facts about the local environment
Materials Needed: Scavenger-hunt worksheets, one clipboard for each group, one pedometer for each student (optional), space outdoors with clearly defined boundaries

Preparation:
Create a scavenger-hunt list of plants, rocks, types of soil, bugs, animals, animal shelters, or other elements of the local environment that you have been studying. You may choose to create different lists for different groups of students, but they should all have the same number of items on them.

Directions:
1. Distribute the pedometers to the students and briefly explain how to use them, providing a short time for them to practice counting their steps. If you don't have pedometers, explain to students that they will need to count their steps during this activity.

2. Break students into groups of four or five and distribute the scavenger-hunt worksheets and clipboards. If your students do not have pedometers, consider giving them scratch paper so they can record their steps during each segment of the activity.
3. Review all of the items on the lists that they are to find and discuss the boundaries of the space they can hunt in.
4. Explain that students should not bring the items they find back to the classroom, but rather describe the appearance and location of where they discovered them (this is a variation of the usual scavenger hunt rules).
5. Provide directions for how students are supposed to move from item to item (skip, walk, gallop, etc.).
6. When all the groups have completed their lists, collect the clipboards and return to class. Groups who finish early should total the number of steps each person took, and total the number of steps taken by the group as a whole.
7. Lead a discussion with the entire class about the activity. You may touch on such topics as:
   - different ways to categorize the items on the list
   - which items were the most difficult to find
   - reasons that some groups took more or fewer steps than others

Planet Catch

Purpose: Review the names of the planets, their order in relation to the sun, and the revolving of the planets around the sun
Materials Needed: bouncing balls—one per student (the balls do not have to be the same size), ten cones or floor markers, large open space

Preparation:
1. Label nine cones with the name of a planet in the solar system (Mercury, Venus, Earth, Mars, Jupiter, Saturn, Uranus, Neptune, Pluto) and label the tenth cone as the sun. Include on the label for the planet cones a number to represent their order in relation to distance from the sun.
2. Place the sun cone in the center of the open space and arrange the other cones in a line in order of their distance from the sun. Leave enough space between the cones so groups of students could walk between them without bumping into each other.

Directions:
1. Distribute the balls to the students and keep one for yourself.
2. Explain to the class that when you call out a planet, they are to bounce their ball in relation to that planet's relative order in distance from the sun. For example, if you called out, "Mercury," students would bounce

their balls once. If you called out "Saturn," they would bounce their balls five times.

3. Count aloud as you bounce your ball along with the class.

4. Vary the activity by bouncing your ball and counting aloud to a certain number, and then asking students what planet would be represented by that number of bounces. Then, have everyone bounce their balls that number of times.

5. Once the students are completely familiar with the order of the planets, divide them into nine groups.

6. Send each group to line up behind (or next to) the cone of a planet.

7. Have students represent the orbits of the planets while walking in a circle around the sun cone. Remind them that planets stay more or less the same distance away from the sun as they orbit; you may have to demonstrate the different distances from the cone of one or two orbits by walking around the sun yourself.

8. At your signal, have students bounce and catch their ball as they walk their orbits around the sun cone.

9. After all the students have had a chance to make a few orbits, have them sit in place and lead a class discussion on the following topics:
   - The difference in time it takes for the planets to make one orbit (students at the Mercury cone will be walking in small circles than the students at the Pluto cone)
   - The varying effect of the sun's light and heat on planets depending on their distance from the sun

Variation:
Have children rotate their bodies as they walk their orbit to represent day and night.

Creature Feature

Purpose: Simulate the movement of ocean creatures
Materials Needed: Scooters (modify if necessary), ropes, mats, variety of balls

Directions:
1. Put students into groups of three or four.
2. Ask the groups to recall a sea creature they learned about during an ocean unit or lesson on marine biology.
3. Tell students they will be required to work as a group to reenact the animal's movements and behaviors. For example, if a group chose the sea star, they might demonstrate how it moves to capture prey. A sea lion, octopus, crab, wetland bird, or fish might be the selection of another group.
4. Have a representative from each group select a piece of equipment from the selection you have prepared.

5. Give students time to work out and practice their movements.
6. When students are comfortable simulating the movements of the animals, have them demonstrate and explain their simulations to the rest of the class.
7. Engage the entire class a discussion about the activity, including what they decided to represent and how their animals differed from those of other groups.

Oxygen Chase

Purpose: Simulate the flow and oxygenation of the blood, and its use in the body

Materials Needed: One flag belt per student (optional); one red flag per student; extra red flags; poster or sign material; obstacle course props, like foam noodles, cones, hula hoops, hurdles, etc. (whatever you have on hand); large open space

Preparation:
1. Divide the playing area into three sections: one large, open area with clearly defined boundaries that represents the body and two smaller areas representing the heart and lungs.
2. Build an obstacle course with six paths using the materials you have selected. The following is an example of an obstacle course you might set up:

> Path 1: A tunnel made of foam noodle arches with a blue sign that says, "From the Body to the Right Atrium—Crawl"
>
> Path 2: A series of hula hoops flat on the floor with a blue sign that says, "To the Right Ventricle—Hop"
>
> Path 3: A zigzagging path with a white sign that says, "Enter the Lungs and Reoxygenate—Skip" (Place a bucket and extra flags at the end of this path.)
>
> Path 4: A straight path with a red sign that says, "To the Left Atrium—Jog"
>
> Path 5: A hurdle with a red sign that says, "To the Left Ventricle—Move Fast"
>
> Path 6: Another hurdle with a red sign that says, "Return to the Body—Move Fast"

Directions:
1. Teach a lesson on the oxygenation of blood and its flow through the heart, lungs, and the rest of the body. The activity may be played later that day to cement the knowledge, or on another day as a review. It may also be played as an introduction to the lesson.
2. Select four to six students to act as "Muscles" (taggers). Give each Muscle one flag belt.

3. Distribute one flag belt and one flag to the rest of students. (Substitute socks or scarves for the flags, if necessary.) These students are "Oxygenated Blood" and must avoid having their flags taken by the Muscles. The flags represent oxygen.
4. Place the extra flags in the bucket in the "lungs" area.
5. Spread the students out in the "body" area and start the game of tag. If a Muscle takes a flag from an Oxygenated Blood, the player becomes "Deoxygenated Blood" and must travel through the "heart" to the "lungs" to retrieve more oxygen (another flag). Once they have gotten a flag, they are "Reoxygenated Blood" and can return to the "body" to resume the game of tag.
6. Change Muscles every few minutes so all players have the chance to travel through the obstacle course and simulate the flow of blood through the body.

Hoop It Up

Purpose: Identify the bones of the human body
Materials Needed: One hula hoop per student

Directions:
1. Teach a lesson about the human skeletal system. The activity may be played later that day to cement the knowledge, or on another day as a review.
2. Distribute the hula hoops.
3. As you call out the name of a bone, students twirl the hula hoop using the part of the body that contains that bone. (Realize that not every student will be able to twirl the hula hoop with every part of their body, but everyone should have fun trying!)

Pulse

Purpose: Demonstrate effect of inactivity on heart rate

Materials Needed: A clock; paper and pencil for each student; a variety of music with different tempos, from lively to relaxing; open space to spread out in

Directions:
1. Have students find their own personal space in the center of the activity area and sit down.
2. Demonstrate to students how to find and determine their pulse rate.
3. Distribute the pencils and paper.
4. Play slow-tempo, relaxing music and encourage students to sit and rest as relaxed as possible for a few moments.
5. Stop the music and have students take their pulse for ten seconds.
6. Tell students to multiply their pulse count by six to determine their pulse rate per minute.
7. Ask students to stand and move to the perimeter of the activity area.
8. Play fast-tempo music and ask students to skip or jog around the perimeter of the activity area for a few minutes.
9. Stop the music and have students immediately take their pulse again, then find their paper and record it.
10. Take a few more pulse measurements by playing increasingly slow-paced music and having students move in calmer and slower ways (from jogging to walking briskly to walking slowly, etc.). Have students track and record their pulse after each interval.
11. Have students measure their pulses one last time after sitting down for a few moments, and then lead them in a discussion about what they have observed.

Action-Packed Social Studies

A House Divided

Purpose: Review the Union and Confederate states of the Civil War
Materials Needed: One paper plate per student, large open area

Preparation:
On each paper plate, write the name of a state from the Civil War era. Depending on the number of students in your class, some states may be repeated. Scatter the plates facedown in the center of the open area.

Directions:
1. Send half the students to one side of the play area and the other half to the opposite side. Designate one group the "Union" and the other group the "Confederacy."
2. Explain the rules of the game: Each group sends one person at a time to collect a plate from the center of the room without looking at it, bring it back to the group, and decide if it is a Confederate state or a Union state—all without speaking. The groups keep the states that belong to their side and return the ones that don't, leaving them facedown on the floor as they found them.
3. Start the game. The first group to collect all their states wins.

Creative Continents

Purpose: Review important facts about each of the continents

Materials Needed: Blank index cards, large sheets of paper, various pieces of sporting equipment (poly spots, bean bags, bouncing balls, rope lengths, etc.), large open space

Preparation:
1. Write unique facts about each continent on the index cards—one fact per card. Make enough cards so each student has more than one.
2. Trace or copy the outlines of the continents onto large sheets of paper and spread them around the room.
3. Set up equipment stations around the periphery of the room. Decide what physical skill each station will represent—balancing a bean bag on the head while walking, bouncing a ball as you travel, hopping on one foot from poly spot to poly spot, balancing and walking along the length of a rope, etc.

Directions:
1. Spread students out around the activity area, near the equipment stations.
2. Explain what skill is required at each station.
3. Distribute the fact cards to the students and tell them not to look at them yet.
4. Call on students one by one to read the fact card aloud and decide what continent it refers to. Students will perform the physical skill required by the closest station as they move to place their fact cards on the appropriate continent, and then perform the skill as they travel to a different station to wait their next turn.

Date Mate

Purpose: Review historical dates

Materials Needed: A few decks of playing cards; a list of important dates to review; large, open area; music from the historical era you are reviewing (optional)

Preparation (Optional):
Create a set of large cards or transparencies with the names and dates (and perhaps pictures) of important historical events that you have been studying.

Directions:
1. Put students into groups of six and have the groups sit around the edges of the activity area.

2. Shuffle the decks of cards together and spread them out facedown in the center of the playing area.
3. Tell groups that you are going to announce an historical event and the date on which it occurred (or show them the card). Their task will be to send students one at a time to pick up a card and bring it back to the group (without peeking!), until a group has collected the right numbers to represent the date. Face cards have no numerical value. The first group to match the date shouts, "date mate!"
4. Have students return their cards facedown to the center area after each round.
5. Consider playing music from the historical era while students are gathering cards and between rounds.

Capital Games

Purpose: Review state capitals
Materials Needed: one or two decks of cards; two boxes or trays to collect cards in; several copies of a United States map with states and capitals labeled; tape or easels for displaying the maps; a card/activity "key"; large, open space

Preparation:
1. Make as many maps as your playing area space will allow (six to eight is a good starting point). On each map, highlight or color one state. At the bottom of that map, write the state's name, capital, and physical task (for example, New York, Albany, 15 jumping jacks). Display the maps around the room, in a logical geographic order (maybe east coast states on the right wall, west coast states on the left, central states on the back wall).
2. Create your key. The key will tell students what state to go to when they've drawn a certain card: "Ace or 2? California"
3. Place the two trays side by side in the center of the activity area. In one box, place the deck of cards face down; in the other, turn one card face up to start the discard pile.

Directions:
1. Separate students into as many groups as will be workable, considering the space available and the number of maps.
2. Tell students that their task is to choose a card from the deck, check it against the key, find the correct map, read the state name and capital aloud, and perform the physical movement. When they have finished, they return the card to the discard pile and select another one.
3. If students choose a card that will send them to a repeat station, have them return it to the bottom of the deck and select again. Once they have visited all the maps at least once, they can return to whatever station their cards send them.
4. Play for a set amount of time or until all cards are used.

Variations:
- Consider playing patriotic music in the background during the game
- Expand this activity to include world capitals, oceans, mountain ranges, rivers, or other geographic facts

Target Continents

Purpose: Review the names and locations of the continents, oceans, equator, and the northern and southern hemispheres

Materials Needed: Fifteen cones or large signs; a class set of balls in four or five colors; large, open area

Preparation:
1. Label twelve cones with the names of the continents and oceans, and label the last three cones as the northern hemisphere, the southern hemisphere, and the equator. Include the outline of the continent on the continent labels, wavy lines for the oceans, a horizontal line for the equator, and appropriate semicircles for the hemispheres.
2. Arrange the cones in the center of the activity area, in a logical geographic order.

Directions:
1. Conduct a lesson on the names and locations of the continents and oceans. Play this game immediately after the lesson to reinforce new knowledge or on another day as a review.
2. Spread the students out around the perimeter of the playing area.
3. Distribute the balls to the students so that the colors are dispersed evenly around the circle.
4. Call out one of the ball colors and a physical movement (skipping, hopping, walking sideways, etc.). Students holding that color ball roll it to the nearest cone and follow the ball with the designated movement. When they get to their targeted cone, they touch it and call out its name.
5. Play until every student has visited every geographical location.

School Explorer

Purpose: Improve directional awareness by locating sites and symbols on a map

Materials Needed: Map of school grounds (1 for every two or three students), answer sheets, signs for each site, pens or pencils, tape, string

Preparation:
1. Make three master copies of the school map, including the points of the compass, significant landmarks, and other spots of interest. On each copy, mark six distinct locations with Xs and number the Xs. You should have a total of eighteen locations for three maps.
2. Prepare three master lists of six questions about the current social studies lesson. You should have a total of eighteen questions for three lists.
3. Pair each map with a list of questions for a two-sided master; copy the three masters in three different colors.
4. At each location marked with an X, post an easily seen sign with an answer to the question and a physical task that relates to it. For example, a question might be, "What is the state tree of Connecticut?" The answer is the white oak and the physical task might be to do twenty jumping jacks while spreading your limbs as wide as the branches of a tree. Use tape and string to attach a pen to each sign. Make sure the signs are numbered according to the locations and questions.

Directions:
1. Break students into pairs or groups of three.
2. Give each group one of the three maps.
3. Tell students that their task is to read a question on the back of the map, answer the question, travel to the corresponding location (marked with an X on the front of the map), perform the task indicated, and then write down the correct answer from the sign. When they have done that, they read the next question.
4. Encourage students to visit the locations in a non-sequential order, so the students aren't walking around the school in giant groups.
5. When students have visited all the locations on their maps, they return to class and you check their answers. If time permits, you may decide to give a group another map to follow.

Playground Aerobics

Purpose: Learn to create a map and key

Materials Needed: A large copy of a map of the playground, with legend; smaller copies of the map—one per student; colored pencils or crayons; large, open area

Preparation:
Create a map legend by choosing symbols to represent the different game and play areas on the playground. For example, you might show stairs for climbing on the monkey bars, a picture of a hoop for the basketball court, or a circle of arrows for the merry-go-round.

Directions:
1. Post the large map at the front of the room.
2. Distribute the smaller maps to the students.
3. Have students identify and number the ten places they would like to visit on the playground.
4. Have students spread out in the activity area and mime the actions indicated by the legend and the playground equipment they have selected. For example, they might spin around in place for the merry-go-round, or pretend to bounce a ball for the basketball court.
5. Bring students back to their seats and distribute the colored pencils and crayons.
6. As a class, choose colors for the symbols in the legend and color the maps.
7. Extend the activity by having students exchange maps with each other and taking them out to the playground. At the playground, students will travel in order to each playground area indicated on the maps they are holding and spend a minute playing on that equipment.

Race for the Presidency

Purpose: Demonstrate differences between the Electoral College vote and popular vote

Materials Needed: A cutout of each state with the number of electoral votes written on it; three blank nametags; large, open space with clearly marked boundaries

Directions:
1. Write "Candidate A," "Candidate B," and "Candidate C" on the blank nametags.
2. Select three students to be "presidential candidates" and give them each a candidate tag to wear.
3. Distribute one state cutout to each of the remaining students. Hold on to any extras.
4. Send the "presidential candidates" to the center of the activity area and the other students to one end.
5. Stand at the same end of the playing area with the extra state cutouts.
6. At your signal, the "state" students try to run from one end of the playing area to the other without being tagged by a candidate. Students who are tagged give their state cutout to the candidate and circle around the outside of the playing area to get another state cutout from you. When they have another cutout, they try running across the play area again.
7. Play until all the state cutouts have been captured by the candidates.
8. At the end of the game, have students sit on the floor or at their desks for a discussion.
9. Ask the candidates to count and report on the number of states that they "won" and the number of Electoral College votes that they "won."
10. Lead a discussion about the results, hitting on topics like how many votes are necessary to win in the Electoral College and whether it matters if a candidate wins a certain state.
11. Determine the "election" results and proclaim one candidate the winner!

Captain Capital

Purpose: Review the states and their capitals

Materials Needed: One small ball (foam or tennis ball) per pair of students; paddles (optional); large, scale maps of the United States; large, open area

Preparation:
1. In an earlier lesson, have student pairs create large, scale maps of the United States. Save these maps and laminate them if possible.
2. Post these maps to the walls around a large playing area.

Directions:
1. Put students into pairs and send each pair to a map.
2. Distribute the balls to the student pairs, as well as the paddles (if you are using them).
3. Tell students that they will take turns bouncing the ball on the floor and then hitting it against the map with their hand or their paddle. They are only to hit the ball at the wall once, catching it when it bounces back.
4. As one student hits the ball against the wall, the other student watches what state it hits. The student who hit the ball must name the state and its capital.
5. The students switch places after every bounce.

Variations:
- Give directions to the students about how to hit the ball—left hand, with an elbow, aim for a southern or western state, etc.
- Play patriotic music in the background.

Chasing States

Purpose: Review state capitals

Materials Needed: Large, open space with clearly marked boundaries

Directions:
1. Identify one-third of your students as "It" and spread out all the students in the activity area.
2. At your signal, the Its try to tag the rest of the students. Students who are tagged freeze immediately.
3. A tagged student remains frozen until approached by a "free" student. The free student says the name of a state and the frozen student must name its capital. If the frozen student names it correctly, he or she is free to rejoin the game.
4. Students who give a wrong answer have three options: they can try again, the free student can give the name of another state, or the frozen

student can slide (holding the position as much as possible) to another frozen student and ask for help.

5. Students engaged in the state/capital naming process may not be tagged, nor may an It student wait around for it to finish.
6. Switch roles every few minutes so every student gets the chance to practice naming capitals.

Direction Toss

Purpose: Practice the cardinal directions of north, south, east, and west

Materials Needed: One per student of each of the following items: beanbag, hackey sack, small ball, felt circle, mouse pad (or use four items that you already have on hand); large, open area

Preparation:
Determine north, south, east, and west inside the classroom. Post signs with N, S, E, and W on the walls for reference.

Directions:
1. Have students collect one of each of the items and find personal space in the activity area.
2. Instruct them to place the felt circle on the ground like the center of a compass.
3. Tell them to arrange the rest of their items around the circle as follows: hackey sack to the north, the ball to the east, the beanbag to the west, and to stand to the south. They should put the mouse pad aside for later use.
4. When you call out a cardinal direction, students retrieve the item and toss it gently in the air. For example, if you call out "north," students toss the hackey sack up and catch it. If you call out south, have students jump in place.
5. Once students are familiar with the four basic directions, start calling out northeast, southeast, northwest, and southwest.
6. At these cardinal directions, students place the mouse pad in the appropriate corner, retrieve the two items on either side, and toss them at the mouse pad like a target. For southeast and southwest, students would toss the object and then physically jump onto the mouse pad.

State Location

Purpose: Review the locations of the states

Materials Needed: Fifty pieces of paper with the names of the states printed on them in very large letters; an unlabeled map of the United States on an overhead transparency; large, open space

Directions:
1. Distribute the pieces of paper to students and send them to the activity area.
2. At your signal, students are to move around the area in a specified way (hopping, crawling, skipping, etc.) until they are in an arrangement that reflects the geographic order of the states.
3. When a group of students standing near each other are pretty confident they are arranged in the right relationship, they should put their slips of paper on the ground at their feet and go get another slip of paper.
4. If students seem to need a little help, display the transparency with the map of the United States on it for reference.
5. Play until all the states have been placed.

Variations:
- Play this game with world capitals or other geographic facts.
- Play patriotic music during the game.

State Line

Purpose: Combine balancing practice with identifying states by their outlines

Materials Needed: One long jump rope per student; an unlabeled map of the United States; large, open area

Directions:
1. Distribute the jump ropes to the students.
2. Have students find some personal space in the activity area.
3. Display the map of the United States for reference.
4. Call out the name of a state. Students will use their jump ropes to make the outline of the state that you have named, and then practice balancing by walking along the outline on the rope. Students who fall off must begin again.

Variation:
Increase the difficulty level of the balancing by giving instructions for students to follow as they walk along the rope. For example, ask them to walk forwards or backwards, with both hands on the floor, or while balancing something on their head.

Action-Packed Health

Veggie Pig-Out

Purpose: Encourage children to eat healthy foods
Materials Needed: Blank index cards; one jump rope for each student; large, open space

Preparation:
Write on each card the name of a food, using a mix of healthy and unhealthy foods.

Directions:
1. Scatter the index cards facedown throughout the activity area.
2. Distribute the jump ropes to the students and have the students select a card to stand by (but not to turn it over yet).
3. At your signal, the students turn over their cards. Students who turn over a healthy food pick up the card and jump rope vigorously to another one.
4. Students who turn over an unhealthy food are frozen in place until a jump-roping student tags them. Once tagged, the frozen student must name a healthy substitute for the unhealthy food that was on the card. If they are successful, they may jump rope to another card.
5. As students are engaged and jumping rope, call out instructions for how they are supposed to move through the room (jump with both feet, travel in a zig-zag, etc.). Change directions every few minutes.

Escape Route

Purpose: Emphasize the importance of escape routes from your home
Materials Needed: Jump ropes, mats, blindfolds, cones, and other materials students can use to build an obstacle course (modify accordingly); large, open playing area

Preparation:
Divide the activity area into four distinct sections and distribute the equipment evenly between the four sections. Don't worry about putting the exact same equipment in each section.

Directions:
1. Teach a lesson during your fire safety or personal safety unit about the importance of planning escape routes from your home in case of an emergency, and about the value of a safe family meet-up place outside of the building.

2. Divide students into four groups and send the groups to their own section in the activity area.
3. Tell students that their task is to use the equipment in their area to create obstructions, choose a meeting place somewhere in the room, plan an escape route, and practice moving through the escape route until they can all do it quickly and safely.
4. After the students have had time to practice, have the groups assemble at the start of their path.
5. At your signal, time them as they move through the escape route and meet at their pre-chosen location.
6. Conclude the activity with a discussion about their impressions and the importance of practicing as a group.

Variations:
- Provide blindfolds to the groups and have the students go through the escape route blindfolded (after lots of practice, of course).
- Set a time limit for moving the entire group through the escape route.
- Provide sticky notes that say "door" to the groups to affix to certain obstacles. Before students pass that obstacle, they must check it for heat.

Nutrition Dribble

Purpose: Practice reading food labels and determining the number of grams of fats, proteins, and carbohydrates in a single serving
Materials Needed: Nutrition labels from packaged foods—one label per student; balls—one per student; cones, boxes, or other objects to place on top of labels on the floor; cheerful, up-tempo music; large, open area

Preparation:
1. Make a master document of all the labels. The best way to do this is probably to photocopy them one to a page and alphabetize them.
2. Scatter the labels on the floor throughout the activity area and cover each one with a cone, box, or other easily seen object.

Directions:
1. Teach a lesson about macronutrients, including the different uses of proteins, fats, and carbohydrates in the body and the recommended consumption amounts of each. Play this game immediately after the lesson to reinforce the concepts or on another day as a review.
2. Distribute the balls to the students.
3. Assign to each student a specific number of grams of carbohydrates, fats, or protein. Use amounts from labels on your master list.
4. When the music starts, have students dribble their balls through the playing area, from cone to cone. When they reach a cone, they look under it to read the nutrition label. If the label does not have the amount

of grams of carbohydrates, proteins, or fats that they have been assigned, they should return the label to its place beneath the cone and dribble their ball to another one.

5. When students find a nutrition label that meets their requirements, they should pick up the label, dribble to ball to you, show you the label, state the food, and decide if it is healthy or not.

6. After the successful completion of this task, assign the student another amount of grams of fats, proteins, or carbohydrates. The student then dribbles the ball back to the empty cone, places the label beneath it, and dribbles to another.

Recycling Rock-a-Thon

Purpose: Learn about recycling and practice distinguishing between different recyclable meterials

Materials Needed: Three trash cans or buckets labeled with signs in different colors—one that says "paper," one that says "plastic," and one that says "aluminum;" lots of pieces of clean recyclable materials made of paper, plastic, and aluminum; large, open area

Preparation:
Set the trash cans in the center of the activity area and scatter the recyclable trash on the floor around it.

Directions:
1. Teach a lesson about the importance of recycling and what materials are commonly recycled. Play this game immediately after the lesson to reinforce the concepts or on another day as a review.

2. Spread students out in the activity area and point out the three different trash cans, holding up examples of the kinds of recyclable materials would go into each.

3. Tell students that at your signal, they are to move in a specified way (hopping, skipping, sideways) to pick up a piece of recyclable material and then carry it to the appropriate recycle container.

4. When everyone has deposited something in one of the trash cans, give them instructions for a different movement during the next round.

5. Continue until all the recyclable material has been "recycled."

"Hoppy" Feelings

Purpose: Help students identify appropriate emotions for different social situations

Materials Needed: Six paper plates per student; crayons, markers, or colored pencils; large, open area

Preparation:
1. Determine which six emotions you want to emphasize during this activity.
2. Distribute the paper plates and coloring implements to students and have them decorate the plates as faces that represent the six emotions.

Directions:
1. Have students bring their plate faces to the activity area and find their own personal space. Remind them to stay in their personal space for the entire activity.
2. Tell students to arrange their faces within their personal space so that they are as far apart as possible without overlapping someone else's space.
3. Review the skill of hopping. Spend a minute practicing how to hop in different ways—on one foot, with the body held high, hopping backwards, etc.
4. Tell students that you are going to make an announcement and that they are going to hop to the face that shows the appropriate feeling.
5. Begin with the announcement, "I am having a birthday party!"
6. Continue making statements that reflect the emotions on the faces the students drew.
7. Conclude the activity with a discussion of why it is important to express and recognize emotions, and why not all people respond the same way to the same event.

Heart-Healthy Food Challenge

Purpose: Identify foods that are healthy (or not healthy) for the heart

Materials Needed: Multiple sets of small bins or boxes (three per set); paper in a variety of colors; lots of pictures of food items; hurdles or over/under bars and cones; large, open area

Preparation:
1. Figure out how many groups of four or five you can create in your class. You will need one set of cards per group; each set of cards should be the same. Use different colors of paper for each set.
2. Each card in a set should have a picture of a food and its name on one side with a blank back. If you are using a picture of a candy bar, every set should include a picture of a candy bar.

3. Each group will need a set of three bins labeled "Healthy," "OK to Eat Sometimes," and "Not Sure." Make the bin labels the same colors as the sets of cards.
4. In the center of the activity area, create a large circle out of the hurdles alternating with cones (hurdle, cone, hurdle, cone, etc.).
5. Set up stations for each group by placing the sets of bins around the periphery of the circle. You may want to mark them clearly with a cone or larger sign (also color-coded).
6. Spread all the sets of food cards facedown inside the hurdle circle. Scatter all the different colors evenly.

Directions:
1. Divide the students into groups of four or five and send each group to sit by one of the bin stations at the periphery of the activity area.
2. Explain the three different bins and the kinds of foods that would go into them. Point out that the color of the signs on the bins is their team color.
3. At your signal, groups will send one student to run towards the center circle, crawl beneath a hurdle, pick up a food card in their team color, jump over the hurdle to get out of the circle, and run the card back to the group.
4. As a group, students will decide if the food on the card is healthy or OK to eat sometimes and place it in the proper bin. If they aren't sure, they should put the card in the "Not Sure" bin.
5. Once the card has been placed, the student who has just taken a turn gives a high five to the next person to go.
6. Play until all the cards have been collected from the center of the circle.
7. When all the cards have been collected, have students sit down at their stations and lead a discussion about what foods they sorted into what bins. As a group, address and analyze the foods that were placed into the "Not Sure" bin by any group.

Pigs and Pancakes

Purpose: Incorporate literature and movement into health education
Materials Needed: The book *If You Give a Pig a Pancake* by Laura
Numeroff; poly spots or paper plates—one per pair; large, open area

Directions:
1. Teach a lesson about the foods on the food pyramid, especially the
   grains. Use this activity to reinforce the concepts immediately afterwards
   or as a review on a different day.
2. Read the book *If You Give a Pig a Pancake* aloud to the class. Discuss the
   book as you read and when you are finished, asking how the whole thing
   got started and what food group pancakes fall into.
3. Put students into pairs and give each pair a poly spot.
4. Have the pairs find a space in the activity area.
5. Tell students that they are holding a pancake and must find as many
   creative ways to give that pancake to their partners as they can think of
   (overhand, like a Frisbee, drop kick, roll, etc.).
6. Have each pair demonstrate their wackiest way to the rest of the class.

Variation:
Have students expand on the activity by writing a story in the same vein
about a food from a different food group.

Low-Fat, High-Fat

Purpose: Learn about fat content of different foods
Materials Needed: Pictures of different foods mounted on small pieces
of heavy poster board (about 5" X 5" in siz)e—one or more per student;
large, open area

Preparation:
1. Mount the pictures of food onto the small pieces of poster board. Write
   the food names beneath them.
2. Scatter the pictures around the activity area.

Directions:
1. Bring students to the activity area and have them walk around it as you
   give them directions.
2. Tell students that they are going to select a picture of a food and
   determine if it has a high fat content or a low fat content, and then hold
   it above their heads. Students holding a picture of a food with a high fat
   content should skip sideways; students holding a picture of a food with a
   low fat content should skip forward.
3. At your signal, they put their picture back down on the floor and walk
   around until you tell them to pick up another one.

Variation:
Change the type of movement they make for each round. Announce the new movement as they are walking around the activity area.

Password Protection

Purpose: Teach about staying safe with strangers
Materials Needed: Slips of paper with passwords written on them—one per student; four to six name tags with the word "Adult" written on them; large, open area

Preparation:
Select four to six different passwords (depending on the size of your class) and write one password on each slip of paper. Distribute the passwords evenly.

Directions:
1. Teach a lesson on personal safety, including the technique of having a password to use with safe adults. Use this activity immediately to reinforce the concept or later as a review.
2. Distribute the slips of paper to the students. Remind them to keep their passwords secret.
3. Distribute the "Adult" name tags to student volunteers.
4. Explain the rules of the activity. Students are to move around the activity area in a specified way. Adults will approach the other students and say their password. If the Adult's password matches the student's password, they link arms. Together they move around the room looking for more students with the same password.
6. Play until the Adults have found all the students with their password.

Stop, Drop, & Roll

Purpose: Teach emergency procedures
Materials Needed: Three or four red flags, socks, or scarves (optional); large, open space

Directions:
1. Teach a lesson about fire safety. Use this activity immediately after to reinforce the concept, or later as a review.
2. Have students spread out in the activity area and move around in a specified way until they hear you call "Stop." At that point, the students stop.
3. At your signal, have the students start moving around again until you call "Drop." The students drop. (Have them practice falling safely.)
4. Once the students have dropped to the floor, call "Roll." The students roll three or four times like a log.
5. After a few repetitions of this cycle, have students call out "Stop," "Drop," and "Roll" after you do.

Or,

1. Designate three or four students as "Fire" and give them the red flags.
2. Bring the students to the activity area and have them move around in a specified way.
3. The students with the flags try to tag the other students. When they tag a student, they call out, "Fire!"
4. When students are tagged, they call out, "Stop, drop, and roll," and then perform the movements. Once they have extinguished the fire, they return to regular game play.
5. Switch Fire taggers every few minutes.

© 2005 Jupiter Images Corporation

P. E. for Classroom Teachers

Miss Snyder

After thirty-one years of teaching, Miss Snyder has earned the reputation as the "Most Prepared Teacher" at Conrad Middle School in Colorado. She takes her planning seriously, utilizes her time wisely, and is the first person on campus each morning. She loves her job.

During the last couple of years, however, her teaching assignment has changed. All of the sixth grade teachers are now required to teach P. E. class to their students because of budget cuts. Unfortunately, Miss Snyder hated P. E. as a child and she hates the idea of teaching it now. Instead of fretting and complaining about it, though, she decided to teach P. E. to her class the way she wishes it had been taught to her. This semester, her students participate in activities that promote cooperation, anchor academic concepts, improve aerobic fitness, and in general make learning fun!

Why P. E. Matters

The ostensible purpose for teaching P. E. is that it's the law. Teaching requirements vary by district or state, but likely that a chunk of your school day is legally dedicated to educating the body. With the recent focus on academic testing and hitting all the standards during the day, however, P. E. is often set aside because of the perceived lack of time for it and because it doesn't appear on the standardized tests!

In addition to the physical and health benefits provided by a strong P. E. curriculum, mental breaks from academic study refresh students' minds and release the pent-up energy they store while sitting for long periods of time. Putting their bodies in motion improves their concentration and reduces distractions later in the day. After a moment spent engaged physically, students return to a lesson mentally prepared to learn.

Equipment and Facilities Adaptations

Teachers sometimes balk at the idea of teaching P. E. activities within their classroom's four walls, often because of a perceived lack of resources. They worry about

- a lack of equipment
- finding room for the equipment they can get
- not knowing how to use the equipment they have
- having enough room to play
- not being athletically inclined themselves

Fortunately, an activity does not require specialized equipment or technical knowledge to be fun. All that is required from teachers is that they put kids in motion, make safety a top priority, and keep a lookout for easily obtained materials that they can substitute for traditional P. E. supplies.

Consider the following examples of equipment substitutes:

- socks for football flags
- paper cups for cones
- paper plates for poly spots
- crumpled sheets of newsprint for balls

Before you pass on an activity that seems too complicated for your classroom or your students, first consider how you can modify the game to suit your needs. What ordinary items can you use instead of the specified equipment? What rules do you need to change to meet your students' maturity or ability levels? By how many minutes should you shorten or lengthen the game to fit the day's schedule? With this attitude, any game is possible!

Include as part of any P. E. lesson a warm-up and cool-down before and after the main activity to protect the body from injury and to calm students down for the rest of the day.

A note about the activities: Each of these games and activities requires a large, open space to play in. If you need to take students outside to find space, make sure you clearly define the boundaries of the activity area. Also, use music whenever possible to add energy and excitement to an activity. The activity descriptions below do not explicitly describe music as a required element, but it makes any game more memorable.

Warm-Ups

People-to-People

Materials Needed: None

Directions:
1. Put students into pairs and have them stand back-to-back with their partners.
2. Call out different ways for students to make contact with their partners (elbow to knee, foot to head, side to side, hand to quadriceps, bicep to toe, etc.). Encourage them to remain back-to-back as much as possible.
3. When you call out, "People to People," students find a new partner as quickly as possible. Help students find partners quickly to maintain the fast pace of the game.

To the Rescue

Materials Needed: Bean bags or other soft objects—one per student

Directions:
1. Distribute the bean bags to the students.
2. Have students find their own personal space and balance the bean bags on their heads.
3. At your signal, have students move around the room, gently nudging the people they encounter in order to make the bean bag fall off of someone else's head (without losing the bean bag on their own heads).
4. Students who drop their bean bags must wait in place without touching their bean bags until another student comes "to the rescue." The rescuing student picks up and replaces the bean bag on the first student's head.

Roadway

Materials Needed: None

Directions:
1. Put students into pairs and have them stand one in front of the other.
2. The student in the front is the "Car" and the student in the back is the "Driver." Car students should stand with their eyes closed and their hands stretched out in front of them (for bumpers). Driver students place their hands on the Car students' shoulders.
3. If you feel it is necessary, lead the class in a brief discussion about trust.
4. At your signal, the Drivers "steer" their Cars safely around the room by gently turning their partners' shoulders in the direction they need to go to avoid a collision with another Car or classroom object.
5. After a few minutes have elapsed, tell students to switch places.

Variation:
Combine Car/Driver pairs to make Minivans and then combine Minivans to make Limousines.

Bring to Me...

Materials Needed: None

Directions:
1. Put students into groups of four and have the students number off from 1 to 4 within their groups.
2. Call out a number from 1 to 4. Students with the number that you called should come to you.
3. Give the students a list of three items to retrieve from the members of their group. For example, you might ask for one earring, a pencil, and a belt.
4. The first person to bring all three items to you wins a point for their group.

Variation:
Specify how students are supposed to move around the room (skipping, hopping, walking backwards, etc.).

Neural Connections

Materials Needed: Sheets of newsprint crumpled into balls

Directions:
1. Have students stand in a circle.
2. Introduce a paper ball into the group and have students devise a pattern for throwing it to each other.
3. Once they are comfortable with the pattern and have practiced it a few times, introduce another ball into the group.
4. Have students come up with a pattern for throwing two paper balls around the circle.
5. Keep adding paper balls to make patterns of increasing complexity.

Uptake

Materials Needed: Sheets of newsprint—one per student

Directions:
1. Distribute a sheet of newsprint to each student.
2. Have students crumple their paper into a ball and place it at their feet.
3. Students move around the room, dribbling their balls like a soccer ball (with their feet) and trying to kick their ball to tag another person's feet.
4. Students must be in control of their balls at all times (not more than a couple of feet away from it at any point).
5. When students have successfully tagged another person's feet with their ball, they shout "Uptake!"

Neural Explosion

Materials Needed: Sheets of newsprint—one per student

Directions:
1. Distribute a sheet of newsprint to each student.
2. Have students crumple their paper into a ball and toss it gently onto the floor.
3. Call out a vocabulary word from the most recent unit.
4. After you call out the word, students reach down, pick up a ball, and throw it towards the ceiling as they yell out the same word in unison.
5. Repeat the process, calling out different words and having students find and toss up different balls.

Hand Clap Relay

Materials Needed: None

Directions:
1. Divide the class into two groups.
2. Have each group stand in a circle and choose a starting player (maybe the student with the curliest hair or wearing the most red).
3. The starting player claps his or her hands once. The student to the right claps hands once, and then the next student, etc., around the circle as quickly as possible. If a student claps hands twice, the traveling clap changes directions. Any student who claps out of turn (too early or in the wrong direction) steps out of the circle.
4. Periodically have everyone return to the circle and select a different starting player.

Conga Line

Materials Needed: None

Directions:
1. Have students stand face to back in one long line.
2. The person at the front of the line leads the rest of the people around the room with a creative movement. Everyone behind the leader copies the movement.
3. Periodically send the leader to the back of the line so another person gets to be the leader. Students who don't want to lead can immediately go to the back of the line.

Wiggle-Waddle Relay

Materials Needed: Blank paper, plastic cups—one per team

Directions:
1. Divide students into groups of five or six.
2. Distribute one sheet of blank paper to each group and have them crumple the sheet into a ball.
3. Line the groups up across one side of the playing area. Place one cup in front of each team.
4. At your signal, one student from each team places the paper ball between his or her knees, travels across the room and back without losing the ball, and drops the ball into the cup (without using hands). When the ball is in the cup, the next player retrieves the ball from the cup, places it between the knees, crosses the room, and so on.
5. The first team to finish wins!

Pod Walk

Materials Needed: Hula hoops—one per student, cone or object to place on the floor as a landmark

Directions:
1. Place the cone at one side of the activity area and send the students to the opposite side.
2. Put students into groups of three and give each group three hula hoops.
3. Have students interlock their legs with two of the hoops. If the students stand side by side, the arrangement from left to right would be Student One with left leg inside of the first hoop, Student Two with right leg in the first hoop and left leg in the second hoop, and Student Three with right leg in the second hoop. One of the students on the end should just hold onto the third hoop until it is needed.
4. Have students walk with interlocked legs across the playing area, around the cone, and back to where they started.
5. When a group of students has returned, they should find another group to join with. To join groups, one student with a free leg should put a leg inside of the empty hula hoop and have a student from the next group put a leg into it, too. (Now there will be six students joined by five hoops.)
6. Have the larger groups walk across the activity area, around the cone, and back to start, joining another group every time they return, until the entire group of students is interlocked.
7. Send the large group around the cone and back. Celebrate success with a cheer at the end.

Gotcha!

Materials Needed: None

Directions:
1. Have the students stand in one big circle, with their right palms facing up and placed in front of the student to their right.
2. Have the students place their left index fingers in the palm of the student to their left.
3. On the count of three, the students simultaneously try to grasp the finger that is resting in their palms and keep their own fingers from being grasped.

Variations:
- Play the game with the left palms facing up and the right index fingers in the palms.
- Have students cross their right arms over their left arms, using the right index fingers and left palms, and then their left arms over their right arms, using the left index fingers and right palms.

Birthday Line

Materials Needed: None

Directions:
Have students arrange themselves in order by birthday, without talking or moving their lips. Experiment with other ways to have students put themselves in order.

Aerobic Tag and Chase Games

Scrambled Eggs

Materials Needed: None

Directions:
1. Clearly mark the boundaries of the play area. (Don't make it too big or the game will be too easy.)
2. Gather students inside the playing area.
3. At your signal, students must move around the play area, covering as much space as possible without touching another human being.
4. Vary the ways students move through the space—have them skip, crawl, hop, walk, etc. Check rowdy behavior by positively reinforcing the students who are following directions.

Safety Tag

Materials Needed: None

Directions:
1. Clearly mark the boundaries of the play area. Have students find personal space to stand within it.
2. Designate every student "It" and stress safety and gentleness.
3. Begin a game of tag. Students try to tag each other on the knee. When tagged, students must stand in place with hands at hips until someone comes and gently tags their elbow.

Variation:
Change the ways students tag and unfreeze each other. Try giving each other high-fives or personal compliments or performing dance steps.

Partner Tag

Materials Needed: None

Directions:
1. Clearly mark the boundaries of the play area.
2. Put students into pairs and have them stand back to back in the play area.
3. Tell them that one person will be "It" and let them decide.
4. To play the game, the person who is "It" shuts his or her eyes and spins around ten times. The partner darts around It, trying to stay out of reach but not leaving the general space the two of them have found in the play area.
5. When It tags the partner, they switch roles.

Blob Tag

Materials Needed: None

Directions:
1. Clearly mark the boundaries of the play area.
2. Assign to two students the role of "Blob."
3. The Blob students link arms and try to tag the other students in the game. As students are tagged, they link up and become part of the Blob.
4. When the Blob grows to four students, it divides into groups of two. The number of Blobs will increase until eventually everyone is in a Blob.

Clothespin Grab

Materials Needed: One clothespin per student

Directions:
1. Clearly mark the boundaries of the play area.
2. Distribute one clothespin to each student.
3. Have the students help each other affix their clothespins to their shirts on their backs between their shoulder blades.
4. At your signal, students try to grab as many clothespins as they can without having their own clothespin taken.
5. Let students play for a few minutes, and then give a signal to stop.
6. Have students tally up points for themselves—each clothespin still on the shirt is worth two points, each clothespin in the hand is worth one.
7. Play several rounds of this game. If you wish, keep track of individual scores and declare a winner at the end.

Toe Tag

Materials Needed: None

Directions:
1. Put students into pairs and tell them to find some personal space.
2. Have students stand facing each other with their hands on their partners' shoulders.
3. Assign the role of "It" to one person in each pair. The Its use their feet to tag their partners' toes without removing their hands.
4. When It has successfully tagged a toe, the partners switch roles.

Triangle Tag

Materials Needed: None

Directions:
1. Clearly mark the boundaries of the play area.
2. Put students into groups of four and have them find personal space within the play area.
3. Ask students to number off from 1 to 4 within their groups.
4. Randomly choose a number from 1 to 4—the students with that number will be "It" and the students with the next sequential number will be the person It tries to tag. (If number 4 is it, then number 1 would be the target person.)
5. The three students who are not It hold hands in a circle. It tries to tag the target person and the other three students move around to protect the target person from being tagged.
6. It tries to tag the target person without moving under, over, or through the arms of the rest of the group.
7. When finally tagged, the target person becomes the next It and chooses the next target person (not the person who was just It).

Tire Tag

Materials Needed: Bicycle inner tubes (or hula hoops)—one per student pair; six rubber chickens (or other easily spotted objects, like small balls or bright flags)

Directions:
1. Put students into pairs.
2. Distribute one inner tube to each pair. Both students in the pair should stand inside the inner tube and hold it up about waist high.
3. Distribute the rubber chickens to six pairs. The six pairs with the rubber chickens are "It."
4. At your signal, the It pairs chase and try to tag the other student pairs. If tagged, a pair takes the rubber chicken from the It pair and tries to tag other pairs.

Hot Swatter

Materials Needed: Poly spots or Frisbees—one per group; foam noodles—one per group

Directions:
1. Divide the class into groups of five or six.
2. Distribute the poly spots and foam noodles to the groups and have them find space in the play area.
3. Give the groups the following instructions for how to set up the game: Place the poly spot on the floor and form a circle around it. Each person should stand about five large steps away from the poly spot. Place the foam noodle on top of the poly spot in the center.
4. Have groups select the first person to be "It." You could have them count off and then randomly pick a number, or determine it in a fun way (like who has traveled to the furthest place).
5. It stands at the center holding the noodle. With the noodle, It reaches out and tags the leg of a person standing in the circle.
6. When It has tagged a person, he or she must place (not throw) the noodle on the poly spot, touch the poly spot, and then run to fill the space of the person tagged.
7. When a person is tagged, he or she must run to the center of the circle, pick up the noodle, and tag It with the noodle before It has a chance to take the open space in the circle.
8. If It successfully makes it to the vacant space in the circle without being tagged, the new person becomes It. If It does not make it to the space, he or she must tag a different person and try again.

Bonus Ball

Materials Needed: 55 tennis balls, six buckets (or empty coffee cans)

Preparation:
1. Mark eight tennis balls with the number 1, eight balls with the number 2, eight with a 3, eight with a 4, eight with a 5, and eight with a 6. Mark the remaining seven tennis balls with the letters BB (which stands for "bonus ball").
2. Label the six buckets with the numbers 1 through 6 and place them in a line across one side of the playing area.
3. Scatter the tennis balls across the other side of the playing area. (Make sure they don't roll too far away from each other.)

Directions:
1. Divide the students into six teams with no more than eight players per team.
2. Have the teams line up behind the buckets. The numbers on the bucket become the numbers of the teams.
3. At your signal, the first four players of each team run across the playing area to grab a tennis ball with the team's number on it; then, they run back with the ball, drop it in the bucket, and take a place at the end of the line.
4. When a person drops a ball in the bucket, the next person on the team runs out to find another one and bring it back. (There should never be more than four players on a team running for balls at a time.)
5. After a team has collected five tennis balls in the bucket, players can look for bonus balls (BB) to bring back.
6. When all the balls have been collected, have the teams tally their points: one point for every ball with the team's number on it and two points for every bonus ball.
7. Announce a winning team and celebrate!

Inside Games

Whistle Mixer

Materials Needed: A whistle

Directions:
1. Have students scatter and move around the room.
2. Blow the whistle a random number of times.
3. When the whistle stops blowing, students are to form groups and stand back to back as quickly as possible. For example, if you blow the whistle three times, they need to form groups of three people; if you blow the whistle five times, they form groups of five.

(This is also a good exercise for breaking students into groups for academic lessons.)

Match Mates

Materials Needed: Music

Directions:
1. Have students spread out in the play area.
2. Start the music and have students move around the room at random.
3. Stop the music and have students freeze in place.
4. When the students are still, give instructions for how students should group themselves. For example, you might tell them to form groups by eye color.
5. Play several rounds of this game, varying the ways students move around the room and the rules for forming groups (month of birthday, color of shoes, first vowel in the last name, etc.)

Don't Touch!

Materials Needed: Several hula hoops

Directions:
1. Have students form a large square in the play area. Each side of the square should contain about the same number of students. Students should stand far enough apart from each other so that they can raise both arms to their sides and not touch anyone else.
2. At your signal, the students in two opposite sides of the square cross the center to switch sides. Each side should move as a line (no student should get too far ahead of or behind the others); when the lines meet, students in the lines should cross without touching.
3. After a few practice rounds, scatter the hula hoops in the center of the square to form obstacles. When students encounter the obstacles, they must go around them without breaking the line formation, jumping over them, or touching another person.
4. Add another element of challenge by setting a time limit for each side to switch places.

Pair Finder

Materials Needed: Blindfolds—one per student

Directions:
1. Break students into pairs and distribute the blindfolds.
2. Have each pair of students come up with a unique set of matching names, such as "salt" and "pepper," "peanut butter" and "jelly," "stop" and "go," etc. Each partner adopts one of the matching names.
3. Send each partner to opposite sides of the play area so that one person from each pair is on one side and the partner is on the other.
4. Tell students to put their blindfolds on.
5. At your signal, the students start calling out their matching names to try to locate each other.
6. When partners have found each other, they remove their blindfolds, cheer, and move to the sidelines of the play area until the game is finished.

Barnyard

Materials Needed: One blindfold per student

Directions:
1. Distribute the blindfolds to the students.
2. Have students spread out in the playing area.
3. Tell students to put their blindfolds on and freeze in place.
4. Tell students that they are to secretly choose a barnyard animal (cow, chicken, sheep, horse, etc.) and to think—just think, no noise—about the sounds that animal makes.
5. At your signal, have students start making the sound of the animals they have chosen. As they make the sound, students move around the room, looking for other people making the same sound.
6. When students making the same sound find each other, they link arms and keep making the sound to find other people who have chosen the same animal.
7. When all the students are in groups according to animal, have them freeze in place and remove their blindfolds.

Knots

Materials Needed: None

Directions:
1. Put students in groups of seven or eight.
2. Have the groups find personal space in the play area and stand in a circle.
3. Within the circles, the students join hands with two different people who are standing right next to them.
4. Once everyone is holding the hands of two different people, they must try to untangle the knot without letting go of hands. A knot is untangled when the members of the group are standing in a circle (or in two interlocking circles).
5. After the small groups have had time to untangle a few different knots, combine the groups into groups of fifteen or sixteen, or bring everyone together to make one giant knot.

Jump Rope Challenge

Materials Needed: Jump ropes—one per two or three students; one giant rope (optional)

Preparation:
Establish jump rope stations that emphasize particular jump rope skills. Think of as many as possible—crossing the arms while turning the rope, jumping on the right foot only, jumping on the left foot only, turning the rope from front to back, bouncing once between turns, bouncing twice between turns, alternating feet, etc. Use pictures and labels on signs or index cards to explain what skill students should practice at each station.

Directions:
1. Break students into groups of two or three and send each group to a jump rope station. If there are more groups than stations, have the extra groups find space to stand between stations. Students will take turns practicing the skills at each station.
2. At your signal, have one student start jumping rope according to the skill of the station. Students who are not at a station jump rope in place however they would like.
3. Thirty seconds later, have the next student take the rope and practice the jump rope skill. After another thirty seconds, the third person takes a turn (if students are in groups of three).
4. Rotate the groups through the stations until everyone has practiced all the skills.

Variation:
1. Stretch the giant rope along the ground.
2. Discuss a few hints for successful group jump roping—for example, jump when the rope is at the highest point and how to enter and exit a jumping session
3. Choose two students to act as rope turners for a game of giant jump rope.
4. Have the rest of the students line up near the rope, but far enough away so that the rope turners can turn it without hitting anyone.
5. Have the rope turners start turning the jump rope. Let them get the hang of turning a long rope before sending students to jump in it.
6. Rotate students through the turning rope one at a time until everyone has gone through. Then, send students in as pairs, or in groups of four, working up to the largest number possible for students to jump the rope at one time.
7. During the game, switch rope turners so everyone gets a chance to jump rope.

Push-Up Wave

Materials Needed: None

Directions:
1. Have students hold hands and form a large circle.
2. Once in the circle, the students should drop hands and get into a push-up starting position with their heads pointing towards the center of the circle. If necessary, give instructions about good push-up posture (abdomen muscles tight, hips tucked, back and legs in one straight line).
3. At your signal, students lower themselves to an inch above the ground.
4. Select a student to start the push-up wave by pushing up until the arms are straight. Once that person is up, the person to the right pushes up, and so on around the circle until everyone is in the upright position.
5. The first person who pushed up now drops back down to an inch above the ground, and the wave travels around the circle again as students drop down.
6. Vary the wave by alternating directions.
7. Actively challenge the students to do as many rounds of push-ups as they can.

Group Juggling

Materials Needed: Soft balls (or crumpled wads of paper)—one per student

Directions:
1. Put students in groups of six to eight and have them stand in a circle.
2. Distribute the balls to the groups, giving them one ball fewer than the number of people in the group. One person in the group should keep all the balls at his or her feet.
3. The person with the balls picks one up and tosses it gently to a person across the circle. That person tosses it to another, and then that person another, until everyone has tossed and caught the ball. The group should notice the order of who throws to whom and remember it.
4. Practice the pattern several times until everyone knows automatically to whom they throw a ball to and from whom they catch it.
5. When students are skilled at executing the pattern, the first person introduces a second ball. Now the students throw both balls around the circle in the same pattern.
6. The first person keeps adding balls until as many are in circulation as the group can successfully keep in motion.

Outside/Field Games

Two-Deep Fitness

Materials Needed: 20 cones (or other objects for markers)

Preparation:
Use ten cones to outline a very large circle and the other ten cones to outline a smaller circle inside that one. The inner circle should be large enough for half the class to stand in a circle far enough apart to perform exercises.

Directions:
1. Put students into pairs. If there is an extra person, that person will be the leader. If there is not an extra person, you will be the leader.
2. Have one person in each pair stand inside the smaller circle, facing outward, and the other person in each pair stand across from his or her partner, facing inward.
3. The leader calls out and models a physical movement, like toe touches, for the people in the center circle to perform.
4. As the people in the inner circle do their exercise, their partners jog in formation around the outer circle (they stay in order and do not pass the people ahead of them). When they have completed a lap and end up back in front of their partners, they jog in place until the leader gives the signal.
5. The leader tags someone else to be the new leader, and takes his or her place in either group. (If you are acting as leader, stay the leader.)
6. At the signal, the people in the inner and outer circle switch places.
7. The new leader directs the new inner circle through a different exercise and the new outer circle jogs around them.
8. Continue the activity until everyone has had a chance to be the leader or the students are worn out.

Crows & Cranes

Materials Needed: Flag belts and flags (or socks or bandanas) of two different colors—one per student (you will need enough of each color for half the class)

Preparation:
Clearly mark the boundaries of the playing field. You will need space about one hundred feet deep and fifty feet wide. Use chalk, cones, or other markers to indicate a line dividing the playing space horizontally (what would be the fifty-yard line in a game of football).

Directions:
1. Break the class into two teams. Name one team the "Crows" and the other the "Cranes."
2. Give each team a set of flags and flag belts (one color per team) and tell students to put them on. (If you are using bandanas or socks, have students tuck the bandanas into their belts or waistbands.)
3. Have the teams line up facing each other in rows about fifteen feet on either side of the center dividing line.
4. Call out the name of one of the teams as loudly as you can. When a team is called, the students try to run across the line at the center to the other side of the field (they must cross the outer boundary) without having their flags taken by players on the other team. Students who have their flags taken get a point.
5. When all the students are across the field, have the two teams come back to the center, return the flags, and line up again.
6. Call out the name of the other team; they try to run across the field to the other side without having their flags pulled.
7. After you have played several rounds (make sure that both teams have gotten the same number of turns), ask students to total their points. The students with the fewest points (they had their flags taken the least often) win!

Variation:
Instead of using Crows and Cranes as team names, come up with names that reflect content you have been studying. For example, use "Odds" and "Evens." Instead of calling out the team names, call out a simple addition or multiplication problem. If the answer is an odd number, the Odds run across the field. If the answer is an even number, the Evens run.

British Bulldog

Materials Needed: Flag belts and flags (or clothespins)—one per student

Directions:
1. Clearly mark the boundaries of the play area. Leave room for a safe zone at either end.
2. Select one student to be It.
3. Distribute the flag belts and flags to all the other students (It does not wear a flag belt). If you are using clothespins, students would attach them to their shirts between their shoulder blades.
4. Stress the importance of watching where you are going as you run—students could collide with each other if they aren't careful.
5. Send It to the center of the play area and all the other students to one of the safe zones.
6. When you call out, "British Bulldog, 1, 2, 3!" students try to run across the play area from one safe zone to the other without having their flag taken by It.
7. Students who have their flags taken join It at the center of the play area.
8. When you call out, "British Bulldog, 1, 2, 3," again, students try to run back to the first safe zone.
9. Play until there are more Its than runners.

Dog and Bone

Materials Needed: Towels tied into knots (to represent dog bones)

Directions:

1. Put the students into an even number of groups of five or six people each. You need an even number because teams will face off during this game; teams that face off must have the same number of people on each team.
2. Have two teams line up facing each other about thirty feet apart. Number the students on each team from 1 to 6 from right to left (the 1s and 6s will face each other, as will the 2s and 5s, and 3s and 4s).
3. Place a knotted towel—the dog bone—between the two lines in the center.
4. Call out a number from 1 to 6. When a number is called, both people with that number rush out to grab the towel and bring it back to their place in line without being tagged by their opponent.
5. If a player manages to bring the towel back to the line without being tagged, that team gets a point. If the opponent tags the person with the towel before he or she can return to the line, the opponent's team gets the point.
6. Play until each person has had a chance to run for the dog bone at least once.
7. The teams with the most points win!

Loot

Materials Needed: 30 Frisbees (or paper plates), two large hoops (bigger than hula hoops), colored jerseys or pinnies (to distinguish teams)

Preparation:
1. Clearly define the boundaries of the play area. Include an easily seen line down the center to indicate opposing sides of the field. (This line would be the fifty-yard line in a football game.)
2. Place the large hoops near the center of each side of the field. These will be tag-free zones.
3. Stack fifteen Frisbees on each side of the field, somewhere between the center and back of the field.

Directions:
1. Break the class into two teams.
2. Distribute the jerseys (one color to each team) and send the two teams to opposite sides of the field.
3. Explain to students that the object of the game is to gather all the loot (the Frisbees) inside the hoops on their own side of the field.
4. Discuss the rules of the game:
   - Players run across the line at the center to grab loot from the opposing team's hoop and place it in their own.
   - Players may be tagged while on their opponents' side of the field. If they are tagged while holding a Frisbee, they must return the Frisbee to the hoop and walk back to their own side of the field before doing anything else. If they are tagged before they get a Frisbee, they must freeze in place with their hands on their hips.
   - Players may unfreeze teammates by tagging them on the elbows. If unfrozen, player must walk back to their side of the field before trying to get a Frisbee or untagging a teammate.
   - A team may guard its pile of loot, but from no closer than six feet away.
   - Players may not be tagged while they are on their own side of the field.
   - The hoops represent tag-free zones. A player may not be tagged if they have at least one foot inside the hoop on the opposing team's side.
5. Play until one team has gathered all the loot. If time runs out, declare the team with the most loot the winner.

Tennis Ball Relay

Materials Needed: Tennis balls—one per every three students; cones or markers—two per every three students

Preparation:
Space half the cones down one long side of the playing field and the other half of the cones directly opposite.

Directions:
1. Break students into groups of three.
2. Have each team line up single file behind one cone. After they are lined up, the first person on each team should go stand behind the cone directly opposite on the other side of the playing field. This is not a race—students are just placing themselves for the start of the game.
3. Give one tennis ball to the first people in line in front of the first set of cones (the cones where two people are standing).
4. At your signal, the student with the tennis ball dribbles the ball like a soccer ball (kicking and chasing it) across the field in order to pass it to the teammate waiting on the other side.
5. When the first player reaches the second player, the second player dribbles the tennis ball back across the field to the third player; the first player stays behind.
6. When the second player reaches the third player, the third player dribbles the ball across the field to the first player, and so on.
7. Teams should keep track of how many complete relay cycles they make. When you call time, whichever team has finished the most rounds wins!

One, Two, Pass the Shoe

Materials Needed: None

Directions:
1. Have students stand shoulder to shoulder in a tight circle and then sit down with their feet towards the center.
2. Instruct the students to remove their right shoe, hold it in their right hand, and bend their knees with their feet flat on the ground (like the upright posture of a sit-up position).
3. At your signal, students—in unison—lean backwards until their shoulders touch the ground (the reclining posture of a sit-up position) and tap their shoe on the ground by their ear while saying, "One."
4. In rhythm, the students sit up in unison and tap their shoe on the ground by their foot while saying, "Two."
5. For the last part of the rhythm, students say, "Pass the Shoe," while passing their shoe from their right hand to their left hand, and then sliding it under their knees to the person on their right.
6. Repeat the sit-up/chant sequence until students receive their own shoe from the person on their left.

Silly Softball

Materials Needed: Two tennis rackets, two tennis balls, six baseball bases and two home plates (or mats or bags to use as markers)

Preparation:
Set up two baseball diamonds far enough apart so that two simultaneous games would not interfere with each other—at diagonal corners of a playground is usually best. Each diamond should have three bases, one home plate, and plenty of outfield. Place a tennis ball and racket at each home plate.

Directions:
1. Break the class into four teams so you have two games going on at once.
2. Send two teams to each baseball diamond.
3. Explain how the rules of *Silly Softball* differ from regular softball:
   - Batters pitch to themselves (although someone should still stand in the pitcher's position to catch infield balls).
   - Runners cannot be tagged out at a base. Runners caught between bases return to the one they just left.
   - More than one runner can be on a base at a time.
   - Runners who cross home plate automatically advance to first base again.
   - When every person on a team has batted once, the teams switch places.

- Points are awarded to the at-bat team for every runner that crosses home plate, but they are also awarded to the field team for every runner trapped between bases and every pop fly caught.

4. A game of *Silly Softball* would go something like this:

A batter pitches and hits the ball and runs to as many bases as he can before the fielding team throws the ball back to the pitcher. If he doesn't think he can make it to the next base before the pitcher catches the ball, he stays where he is. If he tries to run to the next base and is caught between the bases when the pitcher catches the ball, he returns to the previous base and the fielding team gets a point. The next batters pitch and run around the bases. Any runner who crosses home plate earns a point for the team and returns to first base for another round. When every player on a team has had a chance to bat, the teams switch places.

5. Play as many innings as time permits, ensuring that teams have an equal number of turns at bat.

Variation:
Silly Softball can also be played with a kickball instead of tennis balls and racquets. The same rules would apply.

Inner Tube Relay

Materials Needed: Bicycle inner tubes—one per every four students

Directions:
1. Clearly mark two lines about sixty feet across from each other. One of these lines will be the start/finish line.
2. Break the students into teams of four.
3. Send two people from each team to the start/finish line and the other two people from each team to the line opposite.
4. Distribute the inner tubes to the teams at the start/finish line.
5. At your signal, one person from each team takes the inner tube and runs across the field to the teammates. One teammate grabs the side of the inner tube and the two players run back across the field. The third teammate takes a hold of the inner tube and all three of them run to the fourth teammate. As a group, all four teammates hold onto the inner tube and run back to the finish line.
6. The first team to cross the finish line wins!

Variation:
Experiment with the number of people on each team—the more, the merrier!

Throw & Run

Materials Needed: Baseball bases and home plate (or cones or markers)—one set per every six players; softballs—one per every six players

Preparation:
Set up several playing fields as modified baseball diamonds. Use the cones to mark the bases and chalk to indicate the foul lines (the lines that run from home plate beyond first and third bases) all the way through the outfield. Place a softball on the pitcher's mound.

Directions:
1. Put the students into an even number of teams of six to eight players each. You need an even number because teams will face off during this game; teams that face off must have the same number of people on each team.
2. Send two teams to each baseball diamond.
3. Explain how the rules of *Throw & Run* vary from regular baseball:
   - The only distinct field positions are pitcher and catcher; every other player is a general fielder.
   - Pitchers pitch underhand to the opposing team, but the "batter" catches and throws the ball (there is no bat).
   - Instead of throwing the ball to a base, the fielding team throws the ball to each player in turn. The catcher is the last person to catch the ball.
   - "Batters" are not tagged out at the bases. Instead, they try to run around all the bases and back to home plate before the fielding team throws the ball to the catcher.
   - After every batter, the players on the fielding team rotate positions so everyone plays every position during an inning; for example, the pitcher becomes the catcher, the catcher becomes a general fielder, the general fielders move down a space, and the last general fielder becomes the pitcher.
4. A game of *Throw & Run* would go something like this:

   The pitcher throws the ball underhand to the batter. The batter catches the ball and throws it as far as she can within the playing field (between the foul lines). After throwing the ball, the batter tries to run around all the bases. The fielding team catches the ball, throws the ball to each player on the team in turn, and then finally throws it to the catcher. If the batter reaches home plate before the catcher gets the ball, the team at bat scores a run. The fielding team rotates positions before the next pitch. Teams switch places after everyone on a team has had a chance at bat.

5. Play as many innings as time permits, ensuring that teams have an equal number of turns at bat.

Variations:
- Play with two soccer balls instead of with a softball. The batter starts with two balls—she kicks the first as far as she can within fair territory and tries to dribble the second around the bases before the fielding team relays the first ball back to the catcher (using their feet only—no hands). All other rules are the same.
- Play with a baseball bat and softball. In this variation, the pitcher throws the ball underhand to the batter. Batters cannot strike out.
- Play the game on a basketball court with a kickball. The corners of the basketball court represent the bases. The pitcher rolls the ball to the batter, who kicks the ball. The fielding team must retrieve the ball, pass it to every player (not necessarily in order), and try to shoot a basket before the batter makes it to home. Making it to home before the ball goes in a basket earns the at-bat team a point; shooting a basket before the player makes it to home earns the fielding team five points.
- Play the game on a basketball court with a lightweight, bouncy playground ball. The pitcher bounces the ball to the batter, who strikes it with one hand. The rest of the rules are the same as the kickball variation above.

Triangle Soccer

Materials Needed: Soccer balls—one per every four students; cones or other markers—three per every four students

Preparation:
Use three cones to mark a triangular playing area. The triangles should be big enough for students to kick and pass a soccer ball between them. Place one soccer ball inside each triangle.

Directions:
1. Break students into groups of four.
2. Send each group to a triangle. Three students will start next to the cones as defense; the fourth student will start outside of the triangle as offense.
3. The players at the cones start the game by kicking and passing the soccer ball to each other across the triangle. After every pass, the students at the cones rotate one cone to the right.
4. As the three defensive players are passing the ball to each other, the fourth offensive player tries to intercept the ball. If the offensive player intercepts the ball, he or she takes over the defensive position at the nearest empty cone. The displaced defensive player becomes the new offensive player.

Variation:

Triangle Soccer can also be played as *Triangle Hockey* with hockey sticks and a puck or ball. All other rules are the same. If you play this variation, it is advisable to begin with a discussion of hockey stick technique and safety (no lifting the stick above the knees, for example).

Soccer Croquet

Materials Needed: Soccer balls—one per every two students; wire coat hangers—nine per croquet course; soccer goal net

Preparations:
1. Fashion wickets out of wire hangers (make them large enough for a soccer ball to pass easily through.)
2. Set up two or three croquet fields so students don't have to wait too long to take their turns while playing. Each croquet field should have nine wickets about thirty feet apart. Number the wickets from 1 to 9 and use your imagination to set up the order of the course.
3. Place the soccer goal at one end of the playing field, far enough away so that students kicking a ball at the goal do not interfere with students playing croquet.

Directions:
1. Put students into pairs.
2. Give each pair a soccer ball.
3. Assign each pair to a wicket on one of the croquet courses. Start them off as far apart as possible, depending on the number of students in your class and the number of croquet courses. Some pairs will start at the first wicket, some at the fifth, but everyone will play all nine wickets before the game is over.
4. Students are to take turns dribbling the soccer ball through the wickets in order (starting point doesn't matter). If a student kicks the ball through the first wicket, the partner kicks the ball through the next.
5. Balls can only be sent through the wickets from one side—the side that the number faces. If a ball goes past a wicket by mistake, the student must dribble it back around to the front before trying again.
6. Each pair makes two complete rounds of the croquet course so that each student gets the chance to dribble the ball through all the wickets.
7. When students have completed the second round, they dribble their ball to the soccer goal and take a shot!

Water Play

PVC Relay

Materials Needed: Six PVC one-inch pipes, six large buckets, six empty coffee cans, a sleeve of paper cups, water

Preparation:
1. Cut the PVC pipes about four feet in length and drill at least twenty holes in each. The holes should be randomly spaced all over the surface of the pipe. When drilling the holes, stop when the drill bit hits the center. Do not drill all the way through the pipe.
2. Prepare the relay area. Place the buckets in a horizontal row about ten feet apart and fill them with water. Place the cans directly opposite the buckets as far away as you like.

Directions:
1. Divide the students into six teams.
2. Send each team to one of the buckets of water.
3. Distribute one paper cup to each team.
4. At your signal, the students use the paper cup to fill the PVC pipe with water. They may only use the cup to pour water into the pipe; they may not use it to block the end of the pipe.
5. Teammates use their hands and fingers to plug the ends of the pipe and the holes. When the pipe is full, they carry it to the coffee can opposite their bucket and empty the water from the pipe into the can.
6. If a team's paper cup tears or breaks, they raise their hands so you can bring them a replacement cup.
7. The team that first fills the coffee can with water wins! Alternately, play for a limited amount of time; the team with the most water in the can wins. Settle disputes with a measuring cup.

Sheet Races

Materials Needed: Six bed sheets, six large buckets, six empty coffee cans, a sleeve of paper cups, water

Preparation:
Place the buckets in a horizontal row about ten feet apart and fill them with water. Place the cans directly opposite the buckets as far away as you like.

Directions:
1. Divide the students into six teams.
2. Send each team to one of the buckets of water.
3. Distribute one paper cup and one sheet to each team.
4. Have students unfold and spread out the sheet on the ground.
5. At your signal, one student fills the paper cup with water and sits down on the sheet. The rest of the team takes hold of the sheet corners and edges and drags or carries the person across to the coffee can. The person with the water empties the cup into the can and they all run back to the bucket with the sheet and the cup.
6. Teammates take turns riding on the sheet with the cup of water.
7. If a team's paper cup tears or breaks, they raise their hands so you can bring them a replacement cup.
8. The team that first fills the coffee can with water wins! Alternately, play for a limited amount of time; the team with the most water in the can wins. Settle disputes with a measuring cup.

Fire Brigade

Materials Needed: Four buckets, a sleeve of paper cups, water

Directions:
1. Break students into two teams.
2. Have the teams sit shoulder to shoulder in two long lines facing each other.
3. Place a bucket full of water at one end of each line and an empty bucket at the other end of each line.
4. Place a stack of twelve paper cups next to the full buckets of water.
5. At your signal, the students at the ends of the line next to the bucket fill one cup with water and pass it down. As soon as one cup is filled and passed along, the first students fill another, and then another, until all twelve cups are in circulation.
6. When the students at the opposite ends of the line receive the cups of water, they pour the water into the empty buckets and pass the empty cups back down the line.
7. Students may hold only one cup of water at a time and one empty cup at a time (although they can hold one of each at the same time).

8. If a cup tears or breaks, the student holding the cup at the time raises his or her hand so you can bring a replacement.
9. The first team to transfer all the water from one bucket to the other wins!

Water Walk

Materials Needed: Six large buckets, six empty coffee cans, a sleeve of paper cups, water

Preparation:
Place the buckets in a horizontal row about ten feet apart and fill them with water. Place the cans directly opposite the buckets as far away as you like.

Directions:
1. Divide the students into six teams.
2. Send each team to line up behind one of the buckets of water.
3. Distribute one paper cup to each team.
4. At your signal, the first player on each team fills the cup with water, balances it on his or her head (no hands!), walks across to pour the water into the coffee can, and runs back with the empty cup so the next person can go.
5. If a cup tears or breaks, the team raises their hands so you can bring a replacement. If the cup tears or breaks after falling off someone's head, that person must refill the cup and try again.
6. The first team to fill the can with water wins.

© Jean-Michel Cornet

Developing an Action Plan

Instead of learning about the world while sitting in a chair, why not have students use their bodies as globes? Put the North Pole at the crown of the head, the South Pole at the feet, and leave the rest up to them! When we utilize our bodies in the academic classroom, learning takes place through the integration of many powerful modalities.

Before you can implement the kinesthetic teaching strategies described in this book, however, you need to organize your schedule and activities. This chapter will help you lay the foundation of a solid movement and learning program. Reflect on the following questions to determine how well you have absorbed the content and philosophy of this book.

- Do I understand the basic functions of the brain and learning?
- Can I explain to my colleagues why movement facilitates cognition?

- Do I have better strategies for getting, keeping, and managing student attention?

- Have I expanded my repertoire of movement activities to use during class?

- Am I more confident about teaching an active and entertaining physical education lesson?

The following checklists are intended to help you identify places in the day you can add action and movement, and help you plan the frequency and equipment needed for them. Deciding what activity you want to do, determining what space and equipment you need, and understanding the rules of the game—in advance—will make it much easier to incorporate movement and stick to your commitment to make changes in your class.

Incorporating Movement into the Classroom

Although the nature of some lessons specifies the most efficient teaching strategy to use, many things can and should be taught by different methods. Every curriculum has enough flexibility for you to be creative and engage the learner physically as well as mentally. Energized and active students learn and remember more, participate willingly, and look forward to new units. The following checklist will help you identify places you can pack action into your classroom plans.

1	Change positions	4 times per class 3 times per class 2 times per class 1 time per class 0 times per class
2	Change states	4 times per class 3 times per class 2 times per class 1 time per class 0 times per class
3	Small group discussions	4 times per class 3 times per class 2 times per class 1 time per class 0 times per class
4	Problem-solving exercises	4 times per class 3 times per class 2 times per class 1 time per class 0 times per class
5	Friendly competition	4 times per class 3 times per class 2 times per class 1 time per class 0 times per class
6	Musical transitions	4 times per class 3 times per class 2 times per class 1 time per class 0 times per class
7	Routines that set academic knowledge to body movement	4 times per class 3 times per class 2 times per class 1 time per class 0 times per class
8	Rhymes or poems that set academic knowledge to music or rhythm	4 times per class 3 times per class 2 times per class 1 time per class 0 times per class
9	Games that use physical objects to set academic knowledge to peer interaction	4 times per class 3 times per class 2 times per class 1 time per class 0 times per class
10	Energizers that increase heart rate and blood flow to the brain	4 times per class 3 times per class 2 times per class 1 time per class 0 times per class
11	Aerobic activity that exercises and conditions large muscle groups	4 times per class 3 times per class 2 times per class 1 time per class 0 times per class

Recess and P. E. for Aerobic Brains

The best games can be ruined by a lack of preparation and familiarity with space and equipment requirements. The following checklist is a tool to help you organize your P. E. lesson for the day, or a group of lessons for the week. You may play more than one game per class, so space has been provided for you to list them all. Be sure to include time to warm up the body before engaging in aerobic exercise and to cool off before returning to regular class lessons.

Game	Facilities Needed	Equipment Required
A._____ B._____ C._____	A._____ B._____ C._____	A._____ B._____ C._____
A._____ B._____ C._____	A._____ B._____ C._____	A._____ B._____ C._____
A._____ B._____ C._____	A._____ B._____ C._____	A._____ B._____ C._____
A._____ B._____ C._____	A._____ B._____ C._____	A._____ B._____ C._____
A._____ B._____ C._____	A._____ B._____ C._____	A._____ B._____ C._____

Conclusion

Instead of treating learners like spectators of education, teachers should actively involve students in the learning process. Understanding the research behind movement and learning and building a catalog of strategies and games for cementing academic ,concepts and content will have a significant impact on the overall productivity of your class's performance. When you make these skills an inherent part of your teaching style, you will be amazed at your students' success and your own renewed inspiration to teach.

So are you motivated to change in your routine? Hopefully, you have a better appreciation for how important movement is to learning, more confidence about leading kids successfully through active movement activities—and that you've lost your fear of teaching quality physical education.

Enjoy your action-packed classroom! Your students certainly will.

Activities List

Bibliography

Abbott, J. & Ryan, T. (Nov, 1999). Constructing knowledge, reconstructing schooling. *Educational Leadership*, 57, 66–70.

Adlard, P. A. & Cotman, C. W. (2004). Voluntary exercise protects against stress-induced decreases in brain-derived neurotrophic factor protein expression. *Neuroscience*, 124(4), 985–92.

Adlard, P. A., Perreau, V. M., Engesser-Cesar, C., & Cotman, C. W. (2004, June 3). The timecourse of induction of brain-derived neurotrophic factor mRNA and protein in the rat hippocampus following voluntary exercise. *Neuroscience Letters*, 363(1), 43–8.

Allen, G., Buxton, R. B., Wong, E. C., & Courchesne, E. (1997, Mar 28). Attentional activation of the cerebellum independent of motor involvement. *Science*, 275(5308), 1940–3.

Allen, Richard (2001). *TrainSmart: Perfect Trainings Every Time*. San Diego, CA: The Brain Store.

Anderson, B. J., Rapp, D. N., Baek, D. H., McCloskey, D. P., Coburn-Litvak, P. S., & Robinson, J. K. (2000, Sept 15). Exercise influences spatial learning in the radial arm maze. *Physiology and Behavior*, 70(5), 425–9.

Ayres, A. J. (1972). *Sensory Integration and Learning Disorders*. Los Angeles, CA: Western Psychological Services.

Black, J. E., Isaacs, K. R., Anderson, B. J., Alcantara, A. A., & Greenough, W. T. (1990 Jul). Learning causes synaptogenesis, whereas motor activity causes angiogenesis, in cerebellar cortex of adult rats. *Proceedings of the National Academy of Sciences (USA)*, 87(14), 5568–72.

Brewer, C. & Campbell, D. (1991). *Rhythms of Learning: Creative Tools for Developing Lifelong Skills*. Tucson: Zephyr Press.

Brink, Susan (1995, May 15). Smart moves: New research suggests that folks from 8 to 80 can shape up their brains with aerobic exercise [online article]. Retrieved May 16, 2005 from *U.S. News & World Report* Web site: http://www.usnews.com/usnews/health/articles/950515/archive_010646.htm

Brown, J., Cooper-Kuhn, C. M., Kempermann, G., Van Praag, H., Winkler, J., Gage, F. H., & Kuhn, H. G. (2003, May). Enriched environment and physical activity stimulate hippocampal but not olfactory bulb neurogenesis. *European Journal of Neuroscience*, 17(10), 2042–6.

Calvin, William (1996). *How Brains Think: Evolving Intelligence, Then and Now*. New York: Basic Books.

Campione, J. C. & Brown, A. L. (1987). Linking dynamic assessment with school achievement. In Carol Schneider Lidz (Ed.), *Dynamic Assessment: An Interactional Approach to Evaluating Learning Potential* (pp. 82–115). New York: Guilford.

Caufield, J., Kidd, S., & Kocher, T. (Nov. 2000). Brain-based instruction in action. *Educational Leadership*, 58(3), 62–65.

Cho, J. Y., Hwang, D. Y., Kang, T. S., Shin, D. H., Hwang, J. H., Lim, C. H., Lee, S. H., Lim, H. J., Min, S. H., Seo, S. J., Song, Y. S., Nam, K. T., Lee, K. S., Cho, J. S., & Kim, Y. K. (2003, Nov). Use of NSE/PS2m-transgenic mice in the study of the protective effect of exercise on Alzheimer's disease. *Journal of Sports Sciences*, 21(11), 943–51.

Clarke, D. (1980). Spinning therapy calms hyperactivity, accelerates physical development. *Brain/Mind Bulletin*, 5(20B), 2–4.

Coulter, Dee (1986). *Enter the Child's World*. Longmont, CO: Coulter Pub.

Dennison, Paul & Dennison, Gail (1995). *Educational Kinesiology In-Depth: The Seven Dimensions of Intelligence*. Ventura, CA: Educational Kinesiology Foundation.

Dickinson, D. (1992). Multiple technologies for multiple intelligences. *The Executive Educator*, 14(Suppl., *The Electronic School*), A8–12.

Dienstbier, R. A. (1989, Jan). Arousal of physiological toughness: Implications for mental and physical health. *Psychological Review*, 96(1), 84–100.

Dustman, R. E. (1991). Aerobics fitness helps cognitive function in aged. *Family Practice News*, 17, 6.

Ehninger, D. & Kempermann, G. (2003, Aug). Regional effects of wheel running and environmental enrichment on cell genesis and microglia proliferation in the adult murine neocortex. *Cerebral Cortex*, 13(8), 845–51.

Fabel, K., Fabel, K., Tam, B., Kaufer, D., Baiker, A., Simmons, N., Kuo, C. J., & Palmer, T. D. (2003, Nov). VEGF is necessary for exercise-induced adult hippocampal neurogenesis. *European Journal of Neuroscience*,18(10), 2803–12.

Frick, K. M. & Fernandez, S. M. (2003, Jul-Aug). Enrichment enhances spatial memory and increases synaptophysin levels in aged female mice. *Neurobiology of Aging*, 24(4), 615–26.

Fritsch, G. & Hitzig, E. On the electrical excitability of the cerebrum (1870). In G. von Bonin (Trans.), *Some Papers on the Cerebral Cortex*. Springfield, IL: Thomas, 1960.

Gabbard, C. (1998, Oct 1). Windows of opportunity for early brain and motor development. *Journal of Physical Education, Recreation, & Dance*, 69(8), 54-60.

Gardner, H. (1995, Nov). Reflections on multiple intelligences: Myths and messages. *Phi Delta Kappan*, 77(3), 200–9.

Gardner, Howard (1993). *Multiple Intelligences: The Theory in Practice*. New York: Basic Books.

Gilbert, A. G. (1977). *Teaching the Three Rs through Movement Experiences*: A Handbook for Teachers. Minneapolis, MN: Burgess.

Greenfield, S. A. (1995) *Journey to the Centers of the Mind: Toward a Science of Consciousness*. New York: W.H. Freeman.

Griesbach, G. S., Hovda, D. A., Molteni, R., Wu, A., & Gomez-Pinilla, F. (2004). Voluntary exercise following traumatic brain injury: Brain-derived neurotrophic factor upregulation and recovery of function. *Neuroscience*, 125(1), 129–39.

Hannaford, Carla (1995). *Smart Moves: Why Learning Is Not All in Your Head*. Arlington, VA: Great Ocean.

Henning, R. A., Jacques, P., Kissel, G. V., Sullivan, A. B., & Alteras-Webb, S. M. (1997. Jan) Frequent short rest breaks from computer work: Effects on productivity and well-being at two field sites. *Ergonomics*, 40(1), 78–91.

Hickey, D. T. (2003). Engaged participation versus marginal nonparticipation: A stridently sociocultural approach to achievement motivation. *The Elementary School Journal*, 103(4), 401–31.

Hooper, J. & Teresi, D. (1986). *The 3-Pound Universe: Revolutionary Discoveries about the Brain—From the Chemistry of the Mind to the New Frontiers of the Soul.* New York: Macmillan.

Houser, L. (2001). Teaching physical education with the brain in mind. *Teaching Elementary Physical Education*, 12(5), 38–40.

Jankovic, S. M., Sokic, D. V., Levic, Z., & Susic, V. (1997, Nov-Dec) [Dr. John Hughlings Jackson]. Srpski Arhiv za Celokupno Lekarstvo (Serbian), 125(11-12), 381–6.

Jensen Eric (2003). *Tools for Engagement: Managing Emotional States for Learner Success.* San Diego, CA: The Brain Store.

Jensen, Eric (1998). *Teaching with the Brain in Mind.* Alexandria, VA: Association for Supervision and Curriculum Development.

Kearney, P. (1996). Brain research shows importance of arts in education. *The Brain in the News*, 3(8), p. 1.

Kempermann, G., Gast, D., & Gage, F. H. (2002, Aug). Neuroplasticity in old age: Sustained fivefold induction of hippocampal neurogenesis by long-term environmental enrichment. *Annals of Neurology*, 52(2), 135–43.

Kesslak, J. P., So, V., Choi, J., Cotman, C. W., & Gomez-Pinilla, F. (1998, Aug). Learning upregulates brain-derived neurotrophic factor messenger ribonucleic acid: A mechanism to facilitate encoding and circuit maintenance? *Behavioral Neuroscience*, 112(4), 1012–9.

Kilander, L., Nyman, H., Boberg, M., Hansson,L., & Lithell, H. (1998 Mar). Hypertension is related to cognitive impairment: A 20-year follow-up of 999 men. *Hypertension*, 31(3), 780–6.

Kindler, A. M. (2003, Spring). Visual culture, visual brain, and (art) education. *Studies in Art Education*, 44(3), 290–7.

Kinoshita, H. (1997). Run for your brain's life. *BrainWork*, 7(1), 8.

Kleim, J. A., Jones, T. A., & Schallert, T. (2003, Nov). Motor enrichment and the induction of plasticity before or after brain injury. *Neurochemical Research*, 28(11), 1757–69.

Kotulak, Ronald (1997). *Inside the Brain: Revolutionary Discoveries of How the Mind Works.* Kansas City, MO: Andrews and McMeel.

Leiner, H. C. & Leiner, A. L. (1997). The treasure at the bottom of the brain [online article]. Retrieved May 16, 2005 from *New Horizons for Learning* Web site: http://www.newhorizons.org/neuro/leiner.htm

Lu, L., Bao, G., Chen, H., Xia, P., Fan, X., Zhang, J., Pei, G., & Ma, L. (2003, Oct). Modification of hippocampal neurogenesis and neuroplasticity by social environments. *Experimental Neurology*, 183(2), 600–9.

Martens, F. L. (1982). Daily physical education: A boon to Canadian elementary schools. *Journal of Physical Education, Recreation, and Dance*, 53(3), 55–8.

McKenzie, T. L., Sallis, J. F., Kolody, B., & Faucette, F. N. (1997, Dec). Long-term effects of a physical education curriculum and staff development program: SPARK. *Research Quarterly for Exercise and Sport*, 68(4), 280–91.

Middleton, F. A. & Strick, P. L. (1994, Oct 21). Anatomical evidence for cerebellar and basal ganglia involvement in higher cognitive function. *Science*, 266(5184), 458–61.

Molteni, R., Wu, A., Vaynman, S., Ying, Z., Barnard, R. J., & Gomez-Pinilla, F. (2004). Exercise reverses the harmful effects of consumption of a high-fat diet on synaptic and behavioral plasticity associated to the action of brain-derived neurotrophic factor. *Neuroscience*, 123(2), 429–40.

Palmer, Lyelle (1980, Sept). Auditory discrimination development through vestibulo-cochlear stimulation. *Academic Therapy*, 16(1), 55–70.

Parnpiansil, P., Jutapakdeegul, N., Chentanez, T., & Kotchabhakdi, N. (2003, Nov 27). Exercise during pregnancy increases hippocampal brain-derived neurotrophic factor mRNA expression and spatial learning in neonatal rat pup. *Neuroscience Letters*, 352(1), 45-8.

Prescott, J. W. (1977). Phylogenetic and ontogenetic aspects of human affectional development. In R. Gemme & C. C. Wheeler (Eds.), *Progress In Sexology. Proceedings of the 1976 International Congress of Sexology.* New York: Plenum Press.

Putnam, S. C. (2003, Feb). Attention deficit: Medical or environmental disorder? *Principal Leadership*, 3(6), 59–61.

Raber, J. (1998, Aug). Detrimental effects of chronic hypothalamic-pituitary-adrenal axis activation. From obesity to memory deficits. *Molecular Neurobiology*, 18(1), 1–22.

Ratey, John (2002). *A User's Guide to the Brain: Perception, Attention, and the Four Theaters of the Brain.* New York: Vintage Books.

Rhodes, J. S., Van Praag, H., Jeffrey, S., Girard, I., Mitchell, G. S., Garland, T. Jr, & Gage, F. H. (2003, Oct). Exercise increases hippocampal neurogenesis to high levels but does not improve spatial learning in mice bred for increased voluntary wheel running. *Behavioral Neuroscience*, 117(5), 1006–16. Erratum in: *Behavioral Neuroscience*, (2004 Apr), 118(2), 305.

Rhodes, R. E. & Courneya, K. S. (2003, Mar). Investigating multiple components of attitude, subjective norm, and perceived control: an examination of the theory of planned behaviour in the exercise domain. *British Journal of Social Psychology*, 42(Pt 1), 129–46.

Richardson, Sarah (1996, Nov). Tarzan's little brain. *Discover*, 17(11), 100–2.

Samples, B. (1992, Oct). Using learning modalities to celebrate intelligence. *Educational Leadership*, 50(2), 62–6.

Sibley, B. A. & Etnier, J. L. (2003). The relationship between physical activity and cognition in children: A meta-analysis. *Pediatric Exercise Science*, 15(3), 243–56.

Silverman, S. (1993). Student characteristics, practice, and achievement in physical education. *Journal of Educational Research*, 87, 54–61.

Streff, J. W. (1978). *The Cheshire Study: Changes in Incidence of Myopia Following Program of Intervention.* In S. J. Cool & E. L. Smith (Eds.), *Frontiers in*

Visual Science: Proceedings of the University of Houston College of Optometry Dedication Symposium, Houston, Texas, U.S.A., March, 1977. New York: Springer-Verlag.

Sylwester, R. & Cho, J. Y. (1992, Dec). What brain research says about paying attention. *Educational Leadership,* 50(4), 71–5.

Teng, E. L. & Sperry, R. W. (1973 May). Interhemispheric interaction during simultaneous bilateral presentation of letters or digits in commissuroto-mized patients. *Neuropsychologia.* 11(2), 131–40.

Uysal, N., Tugyan, K., Kayatekin, B. M., Acikgoz, O., Bagriyanik, H. A., Gonenc, S., Ozdemir, D., Aksu, I., Topcu, A., & Semin, I. (2005, May 5). The effects of regular aerobic exercise in adolescent period on hippo-campal neuron density, apoptosis and spatial memory. Neuroscience Letters, 383(3), 241-45.

Van Praag, H., Christie, B. R., Sejnowski, T. J., & Gage, F. H. (1999, Nov 9). Running enhances neurogenesis, learning, and long-term potentiation in mice. *Proceedings of the National Academy of Sciences (USA),* 96(23), 13427–31.

Van Praag, H., Schinder, A. F., Christie, B. R., Toni, N., Palmer, T. D., & Gage, F. H. (2002, Feb 28). Functional neurogenesis in the adult hippocampus. *Nature,* 415(6875), 1030–4.

Vaynman, S., Ying, Z., & Gomez-Pinilla F. (2004, Nov). Hippocampal BDNF mediates the efficacy of exercise on synaptic plasticity and cognition. *European Journal of Neuroscience,* 20(10), 2580–90.

Vaynman, S., Ying, Z., & Gomez-Pinilla, F. (2003). Interplay between brain-derived neurotrophic factor and signal transduction modulators in the regulation of the effects of exercise on synaptic-plasticity. *Neuroscience,* 122(3), 647–57.

Weikart, Phyllis (2003). *Teaching Movement and Dance: A Sequential Approach to Rhythmic Movement.* Ypsilanti, MI: High/Scope Press.

Weinstein, C. E., Palmer. D. R., & Schulte, A. C. (1987). *LASSI: Learning and Study Strategies Inventory.* Clearwater, FL: H&H Publishing.

Will, B., Galani, R., Kelche, C., & Rosenzweig, M. R. (2004, Feb). Recovery from brain injury in animals: Relative efficacy of environmental enrichment, physical exercise or formal training (1990-2002). *Progress in Neurobiology,* 72(3), 167–82.

Winger, N. & Thomas, M. L. (2002, December 10). State study proves physi-cally fit kids perform better academically [online article]. Retrieved May 16, 2005 from *California Department of Education* Web site: http://www.cde.ca.gov/nr/ne/yr02/yr02rel37.asp

About the Author

Cathie Summerford, MS

Cathie Summerford has engaged learners with action, movement, and music in her dynamic keynotes and workshops. Recognized as a true trailblazer and outstanding author in her field, Cathie's energetic action-packed approach to teaching has livened up learning in countless classrooms around the world.

Along with this current book *Action-Packed Classrooms*, she also authored *PE-4-ME: Teaching Lifelong Health and Fitness*. As an Educational Consultant and President of Fit 4 Learning, Cathie has been recognized as a California Teacher of the Year, National Association for Sport and Physical Education (NASPE) Teacher of the Year, and California School Boards Association (CSBA) Golden Bell award-winning author.

Cathie's experiences in the academic classroom and the physical education arena have provided her with ideas galore to share with others. Her rapid-fire presentations focus on involvement, move quickly, and actively engage the participants. As a result, teachers leave her workshops with dozens of practical ideas and with a renewed love for teaching!

In addition, she has over 14 years of experience teaching all levels, from pre-school to college. Her tried-and-true activities are kid-proof and adult-friendly and always loads of fun. On top of it, she is an Iroman Triathlon finisher!

For more information on workshops or to contact Cathie Summerford directly:

Cathie Summerford
20680 Iroquois Court
Apple Valley, CA 92308
760-961-1727
cathie@fit4learning.com
www.fit4learning.com

Classroom Activators
64 Novel Ways to Energize Learners
By Jerry Evanski, EdD, Foreword by Eric Jensen

Put a new twist on teaching and training practices and invigorate your learners with this handy, pocket-sized guide. Each of the three sections—Environmental, Instructor, and Student—presents specific state-changing activities and the brain research behind them. Strategies can be adapted for any age group, from primary to adult. You'll be amazed how simple changes in the way you present material or arrange the classroom can capture students' interest and keep them focused. Shake things up and see results immediately! ©2004 • 141 pages • Item #1657

Environments for Learning
By Eric Jensen

There are many things you can change in your learning environment to boost student success, from lighting and color choices to noise level, seating, and classroom organization! Packed full of easy-to-use strategies and cutting-edge research, this book walks you through the classroom the way your students experience it—through the senses. Learn how safety, ergonomics, and temperature affect learning; lighting, color, and peripheral stimuli improve performance; noise inhibits or encourages learning; toxic pollutants hinder cognition; and why you should include plants in your learning environment. Read about the "total learning environment" and research on the startling relationship between school facilities and student test scores. There is no such thing as a neutral environment: Optimize your learning environment to optimize student performance! ©2003 • 61 pages • Item #1653

To order these best-selling titles or other brain-compatible learning resources, or request our FREE catalog, call The Brain Store at (800) 325-4769 or (858) 546-7555. Or, visit www.thebrainstore.com and browse our online catalog.